THE HOLY SPIRIT

IS VOLUME

18

OF THE

Twentieth Century Encyclopedia of Catholicism

UNDER SECTION

II

THE BASIC TRUTHS

IT IS ALSO THE

51ST

VOLUME IN ORDER OF PUBLICATION

Edited by **HENRI DANIEL-ROPS** *of the Académie Française*

THE HOLY SPIRIT

By A. M. HENRY, O.P.

Translated from the French by J. LUNDBERG and M. BELL

HAWTHORN BOOKS · PUBLISHERS · *New York*

© 1960 by Hawthorn Books, Inc., 70 Fifth Avenue, New York 11, N. Y. Copyright under International and Pan-American Copyright Conventions. Philippines Copyright 1960 by Hawthorn Books, Inc. All rights reserved, including the right to reproduce this book, or portions thereof, in any form, except for the inclusion of brief quotations in a review. This book was manufactured in the United States of America and published simultaneously in Canada by Mc-Clelland & Stewart, Ltd., 25 Hollinger Road, Toronto 16. It was originally published in France under the title *L'Esprit Saint.* © Librairie Arthème Fayard, 1959. The Library of Congress has catalogued The Twentieth Century Encyclopedia of Catholicism under card number 58-14327. Library of Congress Catalogue Card Number for this volume: 60-13835. The Catholic University of America Library has catalogued this volume based on the Lynn-Peterson Alternative Classification for Catholic Books: BQT184T9v.18/BQT-587.H52. Dewey Decimal Classification: 231.3.

First Edition, October, 1960

NIHIL OBSTAT

Joannes M. T. Barton, S.T.D., L.S.S.

    Censor Deputatus

IMPRIMATUR

                                         BT
Georgius L. Craven   121.2

    Vicarius Generalis, Epus Sebastopolis   H413

Westmonasterii, die XVIII AUGUSTI MCMLX

CONTENTS

CHAPTER I

THE ORIGINAL REVELATION OF THE HOLY SPIRIT

It is spring. Nature is peaceful and nothing seems to stir. Everything is secretly thriving. We are walking along a road. Suddenly, without our knowing whence it comes or whither it is going, a gentle breeze surprises us from behind. Instinctively we look round. Who is there?

It is only the wind, you will say. Yes, it is only the wind. But what is the wind? For modern man, the wind is merely a natural phenomenon; it is explained by the difference in pressure between two places, and this difference in pressure is itself explained by that of temperature, or the movements created by different attractions. The difference: contemporary man, if he does not explain everything, has the feeling that everything can be explained.

But man has not always answered the question in this way. Several centuries before our era, a Peloponesian peasant, or a mariner voyaging on the Aegean Sea, would have quickly recognized the "personality" of this sudden wind. For him all the winds obeyed Aeolus, the god of the winds, who kept them enclosed in vast rock caverns where they moaned and groaned. Each wind had its own name, its proper characteristic and function. The malevolent winds recalled the monstrousness of their father, Typhon, and their mother, the viper Echidna. The benevolent winds, eight in number, carried the pollen of the flowers or else caused rain and fertility, announced the arrival of spring, or again, were propitious to sailors or warriors. They were worshipped by a special cult, particularly Boreas, or Septentrion, the North Wind, the master wind, the one which they sometimes regarded as the very breath from the mouth of Jupiter.

In the past it was the same nearly everywhere. In India, for example, Parjanya, god of the hurricane, "rules over the waters and over all living things, sends rain, ensures fecundity for man, animals and vegetation, and in the face of the storms which he releases, the whole universe trembles".[1]

The children of Israel, staunch monotheists, never "deified" the winds. There is only one God. But the wind is, nevertheless a divinely made phenomenon. It is God who sends it. It is God who is breathing; a benevolent breath if the wind brings the awaited rain and with it fertility, but the breath of God's anger or vengeance if the wind comes from the desert, bringing with it blight, drought and the destruction of all vegetable life. That does not mean, we repeat, that the wind is "material" for the Hebrew, as it is for us. It is, on the contrary, under the elusive form of the wind that the Hebrew represents the supra-terrestrial, the celestial, the divine. Consequently, he instinctively sees the wind as the *Ruah* of God, of Yahweh.

The Hebrew word *Ruah*, which the Greeks usually translate by *Pneuma* and the Latins by *Spiritus* (in English, Spirit), is derived from the verb *Ruh* which designates the action of breathing air, of inhaling, of drawing breath. *Ruah* is the breath of the nostrils, just as *Reah* is an odour, a scent. The relation of certain scents with the *Ruah* of God, was to remain well beyond the beginning (cf. Exod. 30. 36), until, at the end of a long divine tutelage, the believer will have learned what the Spirit of God is: God himself. As for us who have received the Spirit of God, we are, says St Paul: "Christ's incense" (2 Cor. 2. 15).

---

[1] Mircéa Eliade, *Traité d'histoire des religions* (Paris, Payot, 1950), pp. 82–3.

The fullness of the Spirit will be communicated to us by Chrism, that is under the symbol of a perfume.

We need not be surprised at these rather humble and even crude beginnings in our knowledge of God. Man passes through various ages, from childhood to adolescence, which are ordinarily so many stages in his understanding. It is the same with humanity which God progressively instructs, till "the appointed time" (Gal. 4. 4). In the time of Moses, the author of the second account of creation still presents Adam and Eve as having "heard the voice of the Lord God, as he walked in the garden in the cool of the evening" (Gen. 3. 8).

The Holy Spirit has always been the Holy Spirit, because he is God. And God has always been Father, Son and Spirit, even when man was ignorant of all these "processions" in God. But God slowly taught us what he is in himself. In revealing his Spirit to us, at least partially, since we know him here below only as "a confused reflection in a mirror" (1 Cor. 13. 12), God did so from without and from within; from without by the action of the wind and every breath of air, of which he is the ultimate origin despite our ready explanation. And at the same time, God was teaching us within, by the reflection on his own activity which he stimulated among his prophets.

The fact that God sends his breath visibly, as he did at Pentecost (Acts 2. 2), would be meaningless if this breath or wind was not perceived as a sign, having a meaning for those who experienced it. It even matters little whether they at first represent the wind as the act of Someone. Perhaps we can see there only the indication of a humanity which, in some respects, was still in its infancy. Small children spontaneously see or hear persons where there are only things or even nothing. Certain children do not dare to peep under furniture because the shadow frightens them, and they fear something dwells there. To say that the weather is "smiling" or that the heavens "rumble" is only an image for adolescents and adults. But before the child discovers these things for himself, he automatically ascribes to them his own feelings, whether real or possible. So the childlike representation of the wind or breath, in the Bible, would add nothing to revelation if it were only the result of a natural perception on the part of a humanity still in its infancy. But this representation is an occasion, a starting point, which God uses to lead us to an understanding of his secret thoughts and inner life.

On the other hand, it would be equally meaningless for man to reflect on his perceptions, if God was not within him, making him recognize the inner significance of what takes place outside him.

God can, indeed, inspire man without the presence of an external, visible and more often than not extraordinary action, but man cannot manifest this inspiration nor communicate it with any facility. Without the inner inspiration, what takes place outwardly does not bring home to man its meaning, and so man cannot understand it.

The divine tutelage is indeed wonderful: by acting visibly, God shows that he is Master of the earth and the universe and by acting within man he leads man, without doing any violence to him, gradually to understand in his own way what he wants him to know. Revelation in no way sets aside or supplants reason which God created as "a bond between us and himself", as the medieval theologian, Moses Maimonides, so beautifully expressed it. It elevates reason. The Word of God does not in fact remain so far above man that he cannot grasp and understand what is said to him, and gradually assimilate it.

> It is not a secret laid up in heaven, that thou must needs find someone to scale heaven and bring it down to thee before thou canst hear what it is and obey it. It is not an art, practised far overseas, that thou must wait for someone to go voyaging and bring it back to thee before thou canst learn to live by it. No, this message of mine is close to thy side; it rises to thy lips, it is printed on thy memory; thou hast only to fulfil it. (Deut. 30. 12–14.)

We can enter then into the dialogue between God and his people. God, in using the language of his children, makes use of the wind and of every discernible breath, in order gradually to educate them. Even if at the end of this dialogue, the *Ruah* of God, his *Pneuma* or his breath, is so spiritualized that it is identified with God himself, we should still not have learned anything new about the Holy Spirit if we had not all along followed the long process of that spiritualization by means of which God, in leading us by the hand away from the images and words we already understand, wills to teach us something new. Do we not use this method ourselves when we describe the operation of the intellect by words borrowed from the physical order? Thus although "to inspire" means primarily the act of filling one's lungs with air, it can also designate an operation in the mind that is other than teaching, even if the effect is the same. "To express" does not only mean extracting the sap or juice from a fruit or other thing by squeezing it, but drawing out and communicating all that is contained in an idea. Our language would indeed be impoverished if it had only one verb, for example, "to speak", for designating the act of expressing an idea. But verbs such as to grasp, to understand, to comprehend, when they are applied to the operations of the intellect, have specifically different meanings by virtue of their origin in the sphere of visible and perceptible actions

Let us see then what God first made use of in revealing the Holy Spirit.

CHAPTER II

THE BREATH OF GOD

THE WIND, BREATH OF GOD

The first wind (the first *Ruah*), which made a lasting impression on the children of Abraham, seems to have been the one which dried up the Red Sea for the passage of the Hebrews: "All night a fierce sirocco blew and the Lord turned the sea into dry land, the waters parting this way and that. So the Israelites went through the midst of the sea dry-shod, with its waters towering up like a wall to right and left" (Exod. 14. 21–22).

Once Israel was over and the Egyptians were swallowed up, Moses immediately intoned a song of victory: "The waters were piled high through the blast of thy fury; the waves were still, at the sea's heart the depths congealed" (Exod. 15. 8).

The memory of this divine "breath" was to restore hope at times of despair. Isaias prophesied to the exiles in Babylon: "And the Lord will make a desert out of the tongue of sea that flanks Egypt; with the blast of his breath he will threaten Euphrates, dividing it into seven streams, that a man can cross dry-shod" (Isaias 11. 15).

The sacred singers give due praise to God for this great deed:

> The waters saw thee, O God,
> the waters trembled at the sight of thee,
> moved to their inmost depths;
> . . . thy crackling thunders rolled,
> till all the world shone with thy lightning,
> and the troubled earth shook.
> Thy way led through the sea,

> the deep tide made a road for thee,
> and none may read the traces of thy passage.
>
> (Ps. 76. 17–20.)

This does not mean that there were not other famous winds. The wind which put an end to the deluge is of special note: "So God set a wind stirring over the earth, and with that the waters abated" (Gen. 8. 1).

But Israel was not yet constituted as a people, and the memory which it preserved of this liberating wind is, despite all, very intangible. Besides the wind which made possible the passage through the Red Sea, we must mention the wind on Sinai and all the winds of the Exodus.

When God manifested himself on Sinai, he did so in a great thunder-storm. The thunder was the trumpet which heralded him. The lightning called attention to him and all the people were in awe of what was to come to pass: "Morning broke, and all at once thunder was heard, lightning shone out, and the mountain was covered with thick mist; long rang the trumpet blast and the people in the camp were dismayed" (Exod. 19.16).

Israel preserved an accurate memory of this theophony,[1] and throughout the centuries its sacred poets constantly referred to it as the type of the manifestations of God.

> Earth thereupon shivered and shook,
> the very foundations of the hills quailed . . .
> He bade heaven stoop, and come down to earth,
> with a dark cloud at his feet;
> he came, cherub-mounted,
> borne up on the wings of the wind.
>
> (Ps. 17. 8–11.)

> Clouds and darkness about him,
> justice and right the pillars of his throne:
> see where he comes, fire sweeping on before him,
> burning up his enemies all around.

[1] Theophany means a manifestation of God.

> In the flash of his lightning, how shines the world revealed,
> how earth trembles at the sight!
> The hills melt like wax at the presence of the Lord.
>
> (Ps. 96. 2–5.)

An entire psalm was dedicated to glorifying God as the Lord of the thunder-storm (Psalm 28).

This awe-inspiring wind, destined to herald the supreme majesty of him who was to give his law to Israel, was not the only one. The winds of Yahweh, sometimes avenging, at others liberating and life-giving, are numerous. It is a wind from Yahweh that gives the signal for the eighth plague in Egypt, which Moses announced to Pharaoh: "The Lord made a sirocco blow all that day and that night. When morning came the sirocco carried locusts with it" (Exod. 10. 13).

But it was also a wind of Yahweh that freed Egypt from locusts: "The Lord thereupon sent a violent west wind, that caught up the locusts and swept them away into the Red Sea" (Exod. 10. 19).

It was also a wind from Yahweh which brought food to Israel in the desert: the manna and the quails. "And now the Lord sent a wind that brought a flight of quails over the sea and drove them down where the camp was" (Num. 11. 31).

> He rained down manna for them to eat.
> The bread of heaven was his gift to them. . . .
> Next he summoned his east wind from the sky:
> it was his power brought the southern gale,
> raining down meat on them as thick as dust,
> birds on the wing, plentiful as the sea-sand.
>
> (Ps. 77. 24–27.)

Thus it is not to be wondered at that winds proclaim or draw attention to a manifestation of God. The winds are his instruments for blessing or chastising. They express God's tenderness and his protecting closeness, like the breeze, the "Ruah of God", which "brooded over the waters" (Gen. 1. 2) in the very beginning just as a bird hovers over the nest with its young:

As the eagle enticing her young to fly,
and hovering over them,
[Yahweh] spread his wings:
and hath taken him and carried him on his shoulders.
                                    (Deut. 32. 11, Douay Version.)

Or, they are a sign of Yahweh's anger: "One breath, one
blast of the divine anger withers them quite, and they are gone"
(Job 4. 9). "The grass is withered and the flower is fallen, because the Spirit of the Lord hath blown upon it" (Isaias 40.
7, Douay).

God commands the winds. Jesus too, and in such a way that
his disciples "all asked in amazement, What kind of man is this,
who is obeyed even by the winds and the sea?" (Matt. 8. 27).
The apocalyptic prophets foretell the manifestation of God's
anger on the last day by winds:

These . . . shall feel the Lord's vengeance,
a burning desert wind that shall dry up their brooks,
foul their springs, lay waste the store-houses where they hoard
    their treasure.
                                    (Osee 13. 15.)

Here is a river coming upon them in full flood,
driven on by the Lord's breath.
                                    (Isaias 59. 19.)

My people's wanton ways are like the hot wind that blows from
    the desert slopes. . . .
And in return I will summon to my side a wind that blows full. . . .
Alas the day, we are ruined!
Now, Jerusalem, as thy life thou lovest
rid thy heart of guile.
                                    (Jerem. 4. 11–14.)

Is this not already the avenging wind which Jeremias announced at the moment of the exile from Jerusalem: "Drifting
with the wind, the drovers thou once didst follow, captive all
those that once held thy love" (Jerem. 22. 22). Likewise it was

a mysterious wind from Yahweh which carried away Elias and made him disappear from the earth (4 Kings 2. 16).

Let us examine this word *wind* which we have been using. The fact that the Greek translation, the Septuagint, consistently expressed the Hebrew word *Ruah* by *Pneuma*, and the Latin Vulgate by *Spiritus* (Spirit), helps us perceive the whole series of meanings covered by the same word *Ruah*, from wind, breath of air or respiration, breath of life as we shall see, to pure spirit excluding all matter. But this permanence of the word with its different possible meanings should not make us forget its origin and original meanings. The author of the Epistle to the Hebrews can write for example: ὁ ποιῶν τοὺς ἀγγέλους αὐτοῦ πνεύματα, which the Vulgate translates literally by *Qui facit angelos suos spiritus*,—in English "He who makes his angels spirits". But the author of the Epistle to the Hebrews merely quotes Psalm 103 here, where the meaning of the word "angel" and the word "spirit" is without ambiguity. The psalm says in fact: "You who make messengers (*angeli*, ambassadors) of the winds (*spiritus*, spirit)" (Ps. 103. 4).

So we must not forget the fullness of the meaning of the word *Ruah*. Although we translate it by wind, as we did where this first meaning is doubtlessly intended, we should be aware of the disadvantages this translation presents. Where, in fact, the Hebrews use *Ruah* to describe a wind, they visualize a wind which comes from God, a wind from Yahweh, more precisely, a breath from the mouth of God, an anthropomorphism from which the inspired author did not shrink during that remote period of the infancy of the people of Israel—a breath from God's very nostrils: the breath from the mouth of God will carry away its flower (cf. Job 15. 30). "The secret springs of ocean came to light . . . when the Lord threatened them with the breath of his anger" (2 Kings 22. 16).

THE BREATH OF LIFE

The wind, however, is not simply a current of air, it is a

living breath, or at least, the breath of someone living. Thus it is a breath of life, a breath that gives life: "God's spirit made me, the breath of omnipotence woke me to life," declares Eliu in the reprimand intended for Job (Job 33. 4).

For a Hebrew, to receive breath or to receive life are one and the same thing; to breathe one's last breath or to die have the same meaning. Do we not ourselves say of one who is dying that he is breathing his last? But for biblical anthropology this visible act of dying is not only the sign of a life which is being extinguished, it is the very reality of a life that is thus surrendered. Man is composed of two elements, the one earthly, the flesh, which comes from below, and the other, heavenly, which comes from above, the breath which God gives and which he withdraws when he wills: "Back goes dust to its parent earth, and the spirit returns to God who gave it" (Eccles. 12. 7). "As soon as the breath leaves his body, man goes back to the dust he belongs to" (Ps. 145. 4; cf. 77. 39). "All living things that breathe, all the spirits of all mankind, lie in the hollow of his hand" (Job 12. 10). "The breath of life man must resign at last; the day of his death he cannot determine" (Eccles. 8. 8.).

On several occasions Yahweh is called the God "of the spirits of all flesh"[2] (Num. 16. 22; 27. 16, Douay), the word flesh being understood in the individual sense. This opposition between the flesh and the breath of life is continually present in biblical tradition. We find it in St Paul in its completely spiritualized form: flesh and spirit (cf. Gal. 5. 17; Rom. 8. 5–9, etc.).

Life in some respects is a loan from God. God lends, so to speak, a part of his breath and man lives; he withdraws it and man dies: "While life is in me, while he still grants me breath" (Job 27. 3).

---

[2] We find the same among Israel's neighbours; the Egyptian god of air, Shou, gives life to men by a gesture that is identical with that of Yahweh: "I make them subsist and keep life in them by my mouth, I the life which is found in their nostrils; I bring my breath to their throat" (quoted by J. Guillet, *Thèmes bibliques*, Paris, Aubier, 1950, p. 229).

> He has but to turn his thought towards men,
> reclaiming the spirit he once breathed into them,
> and all life would fail everywhere;
> mankind would return to its dust.
>
> (Job 34. 14–15.)

Life is the breath of God in man. God lends it and takes it back at any moment: "Thou fool, this night thou must render up thy soul" (Luke 12. 30).

When God beheld that "the sons of God saw how beautiful were these daughters of men, and took them as wives, choosing where they would", he declared "this spirit of mine shall not endure in man for ever" and he imposed a limit on the duration of their life (Gen. 6. 2–3).

To this immediate dependence on God for life, which the just man expresses as giving back his breath into God's hands at the moment of death (Luke 23. 46; Ps. 30. 6), the Psalmist devotes a beautiful canticle of praise:

> And all look up to thee . . .
> thou hidest thy face, and they are dismayed,
> thou takest their life from them, and they breathe no more,
> go back to the dust they came from.
> Then thou sendest forth thy spirit and there is fresh creation,
> thou dost repeople the face of earth.
>
> (Ps. 103. 27–30.)

It is God, says Isaias, who "gives being and breath to all that lives and moves on the earth" (Isaias 42. 5). But was this not already said at the creation, when God "formed man, breathed into his nostrils the breath of life, and made him into a living soul" (Gen. 2. 7)? Admittedly this verse from Genesis does not mention *Ruah* but *Nesamah*, for the *breath* of Yahweh. However, the two terms are practically synonymous, a fact which the Book of Job brings out in an alliteration well known in the Wisdom literature: "It is the spirit in a man, the breath of the Almighty" (cf. Job 32. 8).

Irrespective of the words used, this is surely the thought of the author of the second creation account and, after him, of the whole of biblical tradition. When Ezechiel was instructed by God to prophesy over the dry bones he was to say:

> A message to these bones from the Lord: I mean to send my spirit into you, and restore you to life. Sinews shall be given you, flesh shall grow on you, and skin cover you; and I will give you breath to bring you to life again; will you then doubt the Lord's power?... Come, breath of life, from the four winds, and breathe on these slain men to make them live. So I prophesied as he had bidden me, and the breath of life came into them, so that they lived again; and all rose to their feet, host upon host of them. (Ezech. 37. 5–10.)

We have stressed the words *breath* and *wind* which *Ruah* signifies. Should it not be translated as *spirit* even now in this prophecy of Ezechiel? We are approaching the point at which *Ruah* will mean "spirit", but the spirit *who gives life* just as the breath gave it and expressed it.

Out of all the texts where *Ruah* still means breath—though in a sense which tends to have become spiritualized—we can, in passing, quote a beautiful passage from Malachias. The prophet is protesting against the increasing number of divorces, due to the introduction of marriage to foreign women, a custom which Nehemias later condemned. Malachias declares:

> And anon, weeping and wailing, you drench the Lord's altar with your tears! What marvel if I heed your sacrifices no more, gift of yours is none can appease me? And the reason of it? Because the Lord bears witness to her wrongs, that wife of thy manhood's age, whom now thou spurnest, thy partner, thy covenanted bride. Yet doer of this is the same man as ever, the will of him is unchanged; he asks nothing better, now as before, than to breed a God-fearing race; to that will, men of Juda, keep true. (Mal. 2. 13–15.)

Thus, according to the prophet, it is one and the same thing to take care of one's own life and remain faithful to one's lawful spouse.[3] But why? Because God made them "one flesh" in the beginning. "That is why a man is destined to leave father and mother and cling to his wife instead, so that the two become one flesh" (Gen. 2. 24). Malachias emphasizes the unique existence of those who exchange and unite their breath of life, of those at least, whose breath of life God himself unites. If before God they are now only one "breath", each one must care for his own life if he is to be faithful to his spouse. "Therefore, no human whim can break the conjugal bond"[4] which aims at bringing forth a posterity belonging to God through the communication of the same "breath" in two beings.

[3] The interpretation which follows is based on that of A. Van Hoonacker, *Les Douze petits prophètes* (Paris, Gabalda, 1908), p. 726.
[4] Ibid.

CHAPTER III

FROM THE BREATH OF THE WARRIOR TO THAT OF THE MESSIAS

We can now consider the various possible qualities of this breath of life. We shall discover a new series of meanings and finally we shall see taking shape the outline of an inner and properly spiritual reality, towards which the divine tutelage is leading us.

We have seen that the Hebrews considered the wind as a sign of God's various moods—if we can so speak—according as he is violent and destructive (cf. Ezech. 13. 13) or, on the contrary, considerate and benevolent to the earth. God's anger and tenderness are expressed by "the breath of his nostrils". These naïve anthropomorphisms of the inspired author are only possible because on a final analysis he knows that man is made "in the image and likeness of God", and he is not afraid to think that God possesses what he finds in man, even if God possesses it in a transcendent manner. What does he see in man?

The breath of a violent man "is as the winter rain", says Isaias (25. 4), one which falls thick and fast in the East and from which man must protect himself. The breath which abates is an anger which is dying down (cf. Judges 8. 3).

Joy has the special quality of reviving the breath. Thus, when the sons of Jacob related to their father what Joseph had told them, Jacob's breath comes to life again. Misfortune, on the contrary, makes the breath fail: "my breath fails me" (cf. Job 17. 1) says Job, crushed by the insipid talk of his "friends" who aggravate his misfortune. Isaias speaks of the weakened "breath" of the forsaken woman (54. 6); a persecutor who wants to call out to God his distress says that "his breath is ready to faint within him" (Psalm 141. 4).

But the abatement of the breath or its amplification does not only signify sorrow or joy. Do we not also speak of admiration as taking the breath away? "And when the queen of Saba saw how wise a man [Solomon] was, saw too, the house he had built, the food that was on his table, the lodging of his servants, the order and splendour of his court, how the wine went round and what burnt sacrifice he offered in the Lord's temple, she stood breathless in wonder" (3 Kings 10. 5).

Terror and fear have the same effect. Rahab, the prostitute of Jericho, gave courage to the assailants of the city by relating to them how the inhabitants had "daunted spirits" (cf. Josue 2. 11; the same expression is found in Exod. 6. 9 and Josue 5. 1) after they learned of the great deeds of the Hebrews. On the other hand, an unrestrained breath can only be the expression of pride and pretension (cf. Eccles. 7. 8).

Is it necessary to here point out the facility of possible transitions in meaning? We can readily appreciate why, in the case of a courageous soldier or runner, we say "he has spirit". But we say it also of a good speaker. We even say it of a writer, a poet, a philosopher or thinker. Imperceptibly, then, "breath" becomes a synonym not only for an inner disposition, but for inner liveliness, inspiration, the heart, the spirit, the soul, the inner immaterial principle of existence and action.

But although it is well for us to perceive the conclusion for an instant so as to discern the direction of the way we are following, we must not by-pass any of the stages. For the moment the breath appears to us in one of its meanings as an inner disposition of man, either good or bad.

THE BREATHS OF MAN

This disposition can be personal or can come from a sort of assumed personality. Thus, when the "breath of Yahweh" took possession of David, an "evil spirit (or breath)" which the inspired author referred to as "coming from Yahweh" (cf. 1 Kings 16. 14) took possession of Saul who began to experience fear. So they sought to soothe him by playing the zither before him. But later, always under the influence of this evil spirit (or breath) coming from Yahweh (cf. 1 Kings 19. 9), Saul tried to "pin David to the wall" with his lance (1 Kings 19. 10). "The spirit is said to come from Yahweh and will be called the evil spirit of God because the Israelites attribute everything to God as the first cause."[1] Thus it is that the Bible speaks to us of God sending the spirit of discord (Judges 9. 23), or the spirit of untruth (3 Kings 22. 19–23), the spirit of confusion (Isaias 19. 14), the spirit of lethargy (Isaias 19. 10), or on the contrary—and what is more understandable—the spirit of fervour, a "gracious spirit" (Nehemias 9. 20; cf. Psalm 142. 10). What we call passing moods or more profoundly the lasting dispositions of virtues and vices, the ancients instinctively represented as inner breaths or spirits, often moreover attributed to angels. This anthropology was for long common among the Fathers of the Church and the theologians of the first centuries. The biblical conception of man is not an "individualist" conception. The inspired authors consider man as the centre of a network of innumerable relations with other "spirits" whose absolute Master is God (cf. Psalm 103. 3–4).

The "breaths" or "spirits" of man to which we have just referred are inner dispositions which affect activity. It is in reference to definite acts that man is said to have a great deal of breath or, on the contrary, to have only a weak breath, a slower breath, a broken breath. According as the quality of

[1] *La sainte Bible* translated under the direction of the Biblical School at Jerusalem, Paris (Editions du Cerf, 1956), p. 295, in the note on 1 Samuel 16. 14.

the envisaged act is physical, spiritual or mixed, the meaning of breath will, therefore, be more or less coarse or spiritual.

THE BREATH OF THE WARRIOR

In the time of the Judges, for example, the "breath" given to man is still only a warlike breath, for strife and victory. Thus, when the "spirit of the Lord wrapped Gideon round, one blast of his horn rallied Abiezer's clan behind him" (Judges 6. 34) and he was victorious in the camp of Madian. When the breath of Yahweh took possession of Jephte (Judges 11. 29), he "offered battle to the sons of Ammon, and the Lord gave him the mastery over them" (Judges 11. 32).

The story of Samson killing a lion is still more typical and characteristic of the power attributed to the breath of Yahweh. "So with his father and mother, Samson went to Thamnatha again. And now they had reached the vineyards belonging to the town when of a sudden he met a lion that roared upon him savagely. Thereupon the spirit of the Lord came down upon Samson, and although he had no weapon, he tore it to pieces as easily as if it had been a kid" (Judges 14. 5–6). Somewhat later, when the men of Juda who feared the Philistines wanted to hand him over to them as a hostage and had tied him with ropes, "the spirit of the Lord came upon him and his bonds parted and snapped like scorched tow. No weapon had he, but he found a bone lying there, an ass's jaw-bone; took that instead, and killed a thousand men with it" (Judges 15. 14–15).

THE BREATH OF THE ARTIST, THE SOOTHSAYER, THE KING

But the breath of Yahweh does not only give courage and strength. The author of the book of Exodus relates what the Lord said to Moses: "Thou shalt have sacred vestments made for thy brother Aaron, to his honour and adornment, bidding all those cunning workmen, whose art is the art of the spirit, so clothe him as to set him apart for my service" (28. 2–3). The skill of the artisans who fashioned the priestly vestments is also the result of Yahweh's breath. For the construction of the sanctuary, Yahweh fills "Beseleel, son of Uri, son of Hur", with his breath, and this breath "makes him wise, adroit and skilful in every kind of craftsmanship; so that he can design whatever is to be designed in gold, silver and bronze, carve both stone and jewel and woods of all sorts" (Exod. 31. 3–4; cf. also Exod. 35. 31).

The breath of God gives strength and courage to the war-chief who sets out to deliver Israel, skill to the artisan who works for the Lord. Likewise it gives discernment to certain Judges (Num. 11. 17), to Joseph the power to interpret dreams (Gen. 41. 38). It also gives the ability to govern well: when Samuel was in the presence of David whose name means "commander", he anointed him with oil and "on David, the spirit of the Lord came down ever after that day" (1 Kings 16. 13).

When the people of God were prepared for it, the breath of Yahweh was to make itself known by still other deeds. It was the breath of Yahweh that inspired the prophets, opened their mouths and in some way constrained them to speak. It gave also a good spirit, the virtues.

THE BREATH OF THE PROPHET

Many of the pagan nations in antiquity had their inspired men who claimed to speak in the name of their gods. Thus Jezabel brought from Tyre "Baal's four hundred and fifty prophets" (3 Kings 18. 19) whom the prophet Elias confounded in a famous contest. Likewise, we know through the message which Jeremias sent to "the kings of Edom, Moab, Ammon, Tyre and Sidon" (Jerem. 27. 3) at the beginning of the reign of Sedecias that there were prophets among their peoples. Jeremias calls them diviners, dreamers, soothsayers and sorcerers (Jerem. 27. 9), precisely because they were not prophets of Yahweh and did not speak the truth. They were for the most part unruly ecstatics who gave themselves to all kinds of gestures and went into trances during which they were supposed to prophesy, which does not necessarily mean telling the future but speaking in the name of their god, being the mouth of their god.

This unruly and infectious form of prophetism seems to have been the first form which appeared in Israel, which bears out the truth that in his dealings with men God usually respects the various states of their religious experience, the rhythm of their inner development and reflection, the levels of their social evolution. God in his providence overlooks nothing.

When Samuel "took out his phial of oil and poured it out over Saul's head" (1 Kings 10. 1) to consecrate him the leader of Israel, he foretold to him, so as to give him a "sign from God", the encounters he would have on his way: "So at last thou wilt come to the hill of God where the Philistines have set a garrison; and here, upon entering the city, thou wilt meet a company of prophets coming down from the sacred height. With harp and tambour, flute and zither at their head, they will be uttering words of prophecy" (1 Kings 10. 5). We can compare these first prophets with various types of dervishes. They live in bands (3 Kings 18. 4), mutually excite each other by music and dance and their delirium is contagious (cf. 1 Kings 10. 6, 10). In the times of Elias and Eliseus they form brotherhoods wiser than their brother-prophets (cf. 4 Kings 2. 3–18; 4. 36 ff.; 6. 1 ff.; 9. 1; Amos 7. 14). All together, however, they constitute a primitive form of the religious life and prophetism. If they happen to mime symbolic actions (3 Kings 22. 11) as the great prophets were to do later, it is still difficult to discern when they are moved by the spirit of Yahweh to speak the truth and when they are moved by a lying breath (3 Kings 22. 22).

The genuine prophet is essentially neither an ecstatic and still less a raging, delirious man—although the Hebrew name *Nabi*, prophet, which designates one who proclaims, involves a pun on "delirium" when false prophets are in question—but a man seized by the breath of God to be the mouthpiece of God and to speak in his name. The divine action which consists in possessing the prophet and the prophetic state which consists in being seized by God are so characteristic of prophetism that when Moses declares himself incompetent for the mission God assigned to him, Yahweh told him to choose Aaron to bear the message by "entrusting it to his lips" (Exod. 4. 15). Then Yahweh said: "He shall be thy spokesman, giving out thy message to the people and thou shalt be his representative with God" (Exod. 4. 16). That did not prevent Moses from becoming the greatest of all the prophets, precisely because God spoke with him "face to face" (Num. 12. 8), by a direct communication of his breath.

God's hold is irresistible. "The Lord speaks, who would not prophesy?" says Amos. Jeremias wanted to withdraw himself from this hold, but he could not: "Lord, thou hast sent me on a fool's errand; if I played a fool's part, a strength greater than mine overmastered me. . . . Did I think to put the Lord out of my thoughts, and speak no more in his name, all at once it seemed as though a raging fire were locked in my bosom, till I was worn out and could bear it no more" (Jerem. 20. 7, 9).

We can say that the breath of God lays hold of the prophet from all sides, from without and within. On the one hand the prophet hears a great noise (Ezech. 3. 12), or has a vision (Ezech. 8. 3; 11. 1 ff.) or he is driven to accomplish an action the symbol of which he immediately perceives (Jerem. 18. 3; 1 Kings 20. 2; Osee 1. 3 ff.). On the other hand the breath of God is said "to enter into the prophet" (Ezech. 2. 2). The prophet is aware that he is an instrument and sent by God. He is too forcibly under the divine grasp not to feel it; at times it even goes so far as to induce abnormal yet quite accidental behaviour which places the prophet in something of a secondary state that is not abnormal or depersonalized but supranormal, disclosing to him his superior calling.

The breath which lays hold of the prophet and makes him

hear noises or see strange things is the same breath which is manifest in the winds, or in the life of every man. All these phenomena are related to each other. It is the same breath which dwells within Elias and finally carries him away into heaven in a whirlwind (4 Kings 2. 11). It is the same breath which inspires Ezechiel and makes him stand "upright" (cf. Ezech. 2. 2) in spite of his fear. Warlike strength, power of life, prophetic inspiration, "all this is the work of one and the same spirit" (1 Cor. 12. 11).

So it is not surprising that throughout the life of the people of God, heirs to Moses, like whom "there was never such another prophet in Israel" (Deut. 34. 10), were never lacking almost until the time of Christ. We simply mention Josue, "a man endowed with high gifts" (Num. 27. 18), the prophetess Debbora who has left us a famous canticle (Judges 5), the anonymous prophet of Judges 6–7, Samuel and the communities of brother prophets about whom we have spoken, Gad, David's prophet (1 Kings 22. 5), Nathan (2 Kings 7. 2), Ahias the prophet of the schism between Israel and Juda (3 Kings 11. 29), Jehu (3 Kings 16. 7), the prophetess Holda under Josias (4 Kings 22. 14), Urias under Joachim (Jerem. 26. 20), not to mention those who are referred to in 2 Paralipomena: Semeias under Roboam, Addo under Roboam and Abia, Azarias under Asa, Oded under Achaz.

However, we are better acquainted with the prophets whose oracles in the end formed a canonical book: Amos, the first, who exercised his ministry in the middle of the eighth century, Isaias, Jeremias, Osee, Michaeas, Nahum, Sophonias, Habacuc and Ezechiel. With this prophet of the exile the preoccupation with the last days begins or is at least intensified. It appeared again with greater insistence among the last prophets—Joel, the second part of Zacharias, Daniel. Meanwhile, the author of the Book of Consolation (Isaias 40–55), the prophets of the Return, Aggaeus and Zacharias, then Malachias and Jonas, had considerably enriched the prophetic movement.

A BREATH OF JUSTICE

But in the end the source dries up. It is as though God was withdrawing his Breath for a time. The abuses of the false prophets cause the prophetic institution itself to be condemned: "Banish, too, the false prophets" (Zach. 13. 2), says God, and they now appeal to the prophets of yesteryear: "Bethink you what warnings gave he by the prophets of an earlier day, when Jerusalem was yet safe and prosperous?" (Zach. 7. 7; cf. Dan. 9. 6; Zach. 7. 12). Daniel seems to be one of the last prophets.

Nevertheless, hope lives on. Isaias, Ezechiel, the author of the Book of Consolation, Joel and Zacharias announce a time during which the breath of God will invade the earth like a hurricane. And this will be a breath of justice.

What a great distance has been travelled since the period in the desert and the period of the Judges! The Breath of God was then manifest, or at least allowed itself to be acknowledged only in the wind—a wind of Yahweh's anger or a wind bearing his blessing—or else in the breath of the war leaders, or in the breath of inspired artists, artisans and goldsmiths. Now the Breath of God appears not only as the breath which inspires the great prophets of the Messianic era, but also as a breath of "justice", that is, of holiness, a sanctifying breath. The life which it brings forth is indeed a life from on high, like all life, but it is a life that is supra-human and transcendent in itself:

> My God, bring a clean heart to birth in me;
> Breathe new life, true life, into my being.
> Do not banish me from thy presence,
> Do not take thy holy spirit from me.
> > (Psalm 50. 12–13.)

> The sacrifice God loves is a broken spirit;
> A heart that is humbled and contrite,
> Thou, O God, wilt never disdain.
> > (Psalm 50. 19.)

The Breath of God is holy and good (Psalm 142. 10). It procures contrition, good will, sincerity, steadfastness, purity of heart and at the same time, joy:

> Give me back the comfort of thy saving power,
> And strengthen me in generous resolve.
>
> (Psalm 50. 14.)

> Tidings send me of good news and rejoicing,
> And the body that lies in the dust shall thrill with pride.
>
> (Psalm 50. 10.)

THE SPIRIT (THE BREATH) WILL REST UPON THE MESSIAS

Israel, no doubt, needed to experience many misfortunes if it was to hope for other than visible assistance and an increase of temporal power. How often it experienced the effect of this oracle!

> Out upon you, the Lord says, what treason is this?
> Here be plans afoot that were never mine,
> Webs a-weaving, and the pattern none of my choice.
> Trust me, you do but add to your guilt.
> What are these journeyings down into Egypt,
> And I never consulted?
> Think you to find refuge in the strength of Pharao,
> Look you to Egypt for shelter?
> Strength of Pharao shall play you false.
>
> (Isaias 30. 1–3.)

Thus they "rebelled, distressed the Holy Breath" (cf. Isaias 63. 10; Ephes. 4. 30) of God who "turned their enemy and fought against them" (id.).

But, thanks to God, misfortunes, war, exile, deportation and sufferings of all sorts will have an end:

> All this, until the spirit is poured out on us from above;
> Fruitful as Carmel then the wilderness,

To make your well-tilled lands seem but waste.
Alike desert and fruitful field, the home,
Now, of innocence, the abode of loyalty;
Loyalty that has peace for its crown, tranquillity for its harvest,
Repose for ever undisturbed.

(Isaias 32. 15–17.)

The messianic times which are thus foretold are presented as an era privileged by the "Breath of God". On the one hand the awaited Messias is the one who will be possessed beyond measure by the "Breath of God", on the other, the moment when he comes will be an epoch of an intense outpouring of the divine breath.

In the first place the Messias will be a man completely filled with the Breath of Yahweh:

From the stock of Jesse a scion will burgeon yet;
Out of his roots a flower shall spring.
One shall be born on whom the breath of the Lord will rest,
A spirit wise and discerning, a spirit prudent and strong,
A spirit of knowledge and fear of the Lord.

(Isaias 11. 1–2.)

Thus the Messias who comes from the stock of Jesse, that is, from a weakened family, like a tree whose roots alone remain, will possess what the breath of Yahweh had communicated to Solomon, "a spirit wise and discerning", what was communicated to David, "a spirit prudent and strong", what was communicated to Moses, to the prophets and to the patriarchs, "a spirit of knowledge and fear of the Lord", in other words, the fullness of what Yahweh communicated to his people. Thus were applied to the Messias various names which suggest Solomon's Wisdom, David's bravery, the religious qualities of Moses and the Patriarchs:

Peerless among counsellors, the mighty God,
Father of the world to come, the Prince of Peace.

(Isaias 9. 6.)

We note in passing, since we shall have occasion to return to it, that the Septuagint added a seventh gift to the enumeration of Isaias. This happened owing to a misreading of the beginning of the verse which, in the opinion of the exegetes, is a gloss: "He breathes the fear of the Lord" (Isaias 11. 3).

The Septuagint reads: "the breath of the fear of the Lord filled him". And in order not to repeat the word *fear*, they translated it first by "piety" and the second time by "fear". Thus the list in the Greek text comprises seven gifts: wisdom and understanding, counsel and fortitude, knowledge and piety and fear of the Lord. Inasmuch as the figure seven was the symbol of perfection and fullness for the ancients, in itself the list has an element of truth despite the original error in translating to which it owes its present form. The Church, inspired and assisted by the Breath of God, was to retain this sevenfold list and draw immeasurable spiritual riches from it.

We can now return to the Messias whom this prophecy, quoted by St Paul in Romans (15. 12) and by St John in his Apocalypse (22. 16), presents as filled with the breath of Yahweh. Another oracle in the Book of Consolation comes back to this fullness of the breath which characterizes the Messias and presents his traits of holiness:

And now, here is my servant, to whom I grant protection,
The man of my choice, greatly beloved.
My spirit rests upon him, and he will proclaim right order among
   the gentiles.
He will not be contentious or a lover of faction;
None will hear his voice in the streets.
He will not snap the staff that is already crushed,
Or put out the wick that still smoulders;
But at last he will establish right order unfailingly.
Not with sternness, not with violence;
To set up right order on earth, that is his mission.
He has a law to give:
In the far-off lands men wait for it eagerly.

(Isaias 42. 1–4.)

The Servant-Messias whom these prophetic songs present brings right order upon the earth and teaches men. "He does not flicker" like the flame nor "is he crushed" like the staff. St Matthew was to quote this text (Matt. 12. 18–21), applying it to Jesus.

As for the prophetic poem at the end of the Book of Isaias—

> The Lord has anointed me,
> On me his spirit has fallen;
> He has sent me to bring good news to men that are humble,
> To heal broken hearts,
> Promising the release of captives,
> The opening of prison doors,
> Proclaiming the year of the Lord's pardon.
>
> (Isaias 61. 1–2.)

—it forms the text which Jesus read at Nazareth when the head of the synagogue invited him to do so (Luke 4. 16–19). When Jesus had concluded this reading he said: "This scripture which I have read in your hearing is today fulfilled" (Luke 4. 21).

It is interesting to note the various words in our text which indicate the communication of the breath. Indeed, the breath which "wrapped the prophet round" (Judges 6. 34; 2 Paral. 24. 20) is one kind; completely other is that which "comes" upon him as lightning or the north wind, that which "seizes him" (Ezech. 3. 12–14), which "rests" on him (Num. 11. 25), or that which is simply "on" him (Isaias 61. 1–2). There is here the deliberate statement of a fullness without limit.

THE SPRING OF LIVING WATER

Secondly, as we have said, messianic times are foretold as an era of a collective outpouring of God's Breath. In this regard we have already quoted the oracle on the return from exile in Isaias 32. 15. The prophecy in the Book of Consolation is still more explicit:

> Do not be afraid, my servant, Jacob,
> My true, my chosen people.
> I will pour out water on the thirsty plain,
> Streams over the land that once was dry;
> I will pour out my spirit upon thy race,
> My blessing on thy line,
> And where the grass springs up they shall spring up too,
> Like willows by running water.
> Now, a man will say openly, the Lord's servant I;
> Make his boast of Jacob's name,
> Write with his own hand, Dedicated to the Lord,
> And lay claim to the title of Israelite.
>
> (Isaias 44. 2–5.)

Many exegetes understand these last verses to refer to the conversion of the pagans. In order to manifest their allegiance to Israel, they give themselves symbolic names or tattoo the tetragram Yahweh on their hand (cf. Exod. 13. 16; Apoc. 13. 16). In any case, each one feels that he belongs personally to Yahweh, directly bound to him and immediately taught by him.

In this oracle the breath is related to water. We have already noted the relation between the wind of blessing and the fruitful rain which it brings. When by the prayer of Elias in the time of Achab God put an end to the drought, the author of the book of Kings writes: "The whole sky was dark and clouds came and a wind with the clouds and a great storm of rain began" (3 Kings 18. 45).

The breath of wind is so often associated with a fruitful rain that an antinomy is established between the wind and the desert, and it is the same verb, to pour out, that indicated the descent of the breath (the wind), the descent of water.

> I will pour out water on the thirsty plain,
> Streams over the land that once was dry;
> I will pour out my spirit upon thy race,
> My blessing on all thy line.
>
> (Isaias 44. 3.)

For those who are exiles in the desert, hope for breath and hope for water is identified with hope for the return of life. For those who set out for the country of the north, into exile across the desert, Yahweh says by the mouth of the prophet:

> From the north country, from the very ends of the earth,
> I mean to gather them and bring them home;
> Blind men and lame,
> Pregnant women and women brought to bed,
> So great the muster at their home-coming.
> Weeping they shall come, and I, moved to pity,
> Will bring them to their journey's end;
> From mountain stream to mountain stream I will lead them,
> By a straight road where there is no stumbling.
>
> (Jerem. 31. 8–9.)

Yahweh himself who is the source of life becomes the "source of living water" (Jerem. 2. 13; cf. 17. 13). The two themes, water and spirit, were associated in Ezechiel and later in the prophet Joel: "And then I will pour cleansing streams over you, to purge you from every stain you bear, purge you from the taint of your idolatry. I will give you a new heart, and breathe a new spirit into you; I will take away from your breasts those hearts that are as hard stone and give you human hearts instead. I will make my spirit penetrate you so that you will follow in the path of my law, remember and carry out my decrees" (Ezech. 36. 25–7).

Joel pronounced this oracle which St Peter quoted in his first discourse after Pentecost to declare its fulfilment (Acts 2. 17–21).

> Afterwards I will pour out my spirit upon all mankind [God "pours out" his spirit as one "pours out" beneficial waters]:
> And your sons and daughters will be prophets.
> Your old men shall dream dreams
> And your young men shall see visions,
> Everywhere servants of mine, handmaids of mine, inspired to prophesy!

And never a soul shall call on the Lord's name
But shall find deliverance.

(Joel 2. 28–32.)

We can speak more explicitly of the universal diffusion of
the Breath. It is no longer given to a few—warriors, judges,
artisans, prophets—for a temporal mission, but to all and in
a permanent manner.

The Breath of God, the principle of creation, was also, in
messianic times through the intervention of the Messias, to be
the principle of inner renewal and it was given through the
sign of water. It made each one fit to observe the divine law.
A new heart was to be placed in each man: "One mind they
shall have, and a new spirit shall fill their inmost being; gone
the heart of stone, and a human heart theirs in place of it. My
paths they shall tread, my will jealously obey" (Ezech. 11.
19–20).

It will, therefore, be the principle of a new covenant: "not
like the covenant which I made with their fathers" (Jerem. 31.
32), "this is the covenant I will grant the people of Israel, the
Lord says, I will implant my law in their inmost thoughts,
engrave it in their hearts; I will be their God, and they shall be
my people. There will be no need for neighbour to teach
neighbour or brother to teach brother, the knowledge of the
Lord; all will know me, from the highest to the lowest. I will
pardon their wrong-doing, I will not remember their sins any
more" (Jerem. 31. 33–34). Breath, water, life, covenant, holiness, inner law, new heart—this whole series of words leads us
towards the same reality.

The divine tutelage gradually directs men towards the con-
stitution of a holy people, entirely revivified by the breath of
holiness of a Holy God. However, Zacharias, one of the prophets of the return from exile, was to make it clear that this
will not be without suffering: "On David's clan, on all the
citizens of Jerusalem, I will pour out a gracious spirit of prayer;
towards me they shall look, me whom they have pierced
through" (Zach. 12. 10).

CHAPTER IV

THE INVASION
BY THE BREATH

When the time at which the Messias was to come was fulfilled, it was as though a great wind from God invaded the earth. At each instant, often even with regard to each person with a mediatory rôle, the Breath of God is present.

It is no longer a visible and violent breath as that which enabled the Hebrew people to leave Egypt or that which encompassed the theophany on Sinai. Now it is a breath of life, a breath of holiness, which retains of that breath only the manner in which it is communicated—of coming from we know not where—and its quality of giving life, as the "breath" gives it in Jewish anthropology. It is an invisible and immaterial breath and the life which it creates and imparts is a life that has nothing in common with the life of the flesh:

> No man can enter into the kingdom of God unless birth comes to him from water, and from the Holy Spirit. What is born by natural birth is a thing of nature, what is born by spiritual birth is a thing of spirit. Do not be surprised then at my telling thee, You must be born anew. The wind breathes where it will, and thou canst hear the sound of it, but knowest nothing of the way it came or the way it goes. So it is when a man is born by the breath of the Spirit.
>
> (John 3. 5–8.)

An invisible invasion: thus we can characterize the outpouring of the Breath in the time of the Messias. It is not at all surprising then, even to the attentive eyes of faith, that this invasion should appear in all its fullness only gradually.

THE EYES OF FAITH OPEN ON TO THE INVISIBLE

Peter and Paul

At the time of the first apostolic preaching of which St Peter's first discourse (Acts 2. 14–36) and the first epistles of St Paul (from Thessalonians to Romans) are a testimony, the apostles seem especially aware of the fullness of the divine Breath poured out at Pentecost by the risen Christ. They came to think of Christ as having received a new "Breath" of life at his resurrection, as having been revivified by the "Spirit" and thus as having been constituted the new Adam, the new head of the race, the Messias: "In his mortal nature he was done to death, but endowed with fresh life in his spirit" (1 Peter 3. 18). And St Paul says: "If there is such a thing as a natural body, there must be a spiritual body too. Mankind begins with Adam who became, as Scripture tells us, a living soul; it is fulfilled in the Adam who has become a life-giving spirit" (1 Cor. 15. 44–45).

According to St Peter it was at the moment of the resurrection that Christ was to receive the holy Breath: "God, then, has raised up this man, Jesus, from the dead; we are all witnesses of it. And now, exalted at God's right hand, he has claimed from his Father his promise to bestow the Holy Spirit; and he has poured out that Spirit. . . ." (Acts 2. 32–33). And then Peter concludes: "God has made him Master and Christ, this Jesus whom you have crucified" (Acts 2. 36).

Peter's reasoning is clear. After quoting Scripture at considerable length and in particular Psalms 15 and 109, he was able to conclude that it is by his resurrection that Jesus has been made the "Lord" of whom Psalm 109 speaks and the "Messias" (Christ) to whom Psalm 15 refers.[1] The investiture

[1] See Le Nouveau Testament, translated by the Biblical School at Jerusalem (Paris, Editions du Cerf, 1958), p. 388, note d.

of Jesus as Messias would date, then, from the resurrection
(cf. again Rom. 1. 1–4).

The first "lives" of Jesus

At a later date, though still prior to the compilation by the
synoptics, the apostles pay greater attention to all the manifestations of the holy Breath which preceded the resurrection.
When Jesus himself promised the apostles that they would be
baptized—the literal meaning is "immersed"—in the Holy
Breath as opposed to John's baptism which was only a baptism
"in water" (Acts 1. 5), did this not remind them of Jesus' baptism by John? If the first apostolic preaching laid special stress
on the messianic investiture at the resurrection, through the
divine Breath which Christ henceforth pours out upon his own,
the later catechesis traces this investiture back to the baptism
of Jesus himself. Christ's public life is there presented between
two outstanding manifestations of the divine Breath: the baptism of Jesus and the sending of the Holy Breath at Pentecost
or the mission given to the apostles to go and baptize "in the
name of the Father and the Son and the Holy Spirit" (Matt.
28. 19). It is significant that Jesus, immediately after his baptism, is driven by the Holy Breath to go into the desert. The
presence of the dove, the voice, the waters, the call to the
desert, the kind of temptation experienced in solitude, all this
is rich in allusions full of meaning. The Synoptics presented the
Jordan as the place of the messianic investiture. To this inaugural and prefigurative "pasch" corresponds the "pentecost"
manifested during the ministry of Jesus by his powers against
the evil spirits, by his miracles and by his Word.

Luke and John

On still a third level, which finds its first reflection in Luke,
the early Christian community becomes conscious of all the
manifestations of the Holy Breath which surrounded the very
birth of Jesus. Hence the light of faith casts light on all the
events in the mystery of salvation. The messianic investiture

appears to have been given to Christ as early as the Incarnation. The manifestations of the Holy Breath are, from the very beginning, like a first outline and prefiguring of Pentecost.

In truth, Jesus is the Anointed of God, the Messias, filled with the plenitude of the Spirit of Yahweh from the beginning. But this fullness appears in three privileged moments in the life of Jesus: at his birth, his baptism and his resurrection, and is manifest round Christ at each of these moments. At the first descent of the Breath of God at the Incarnation, it is Elizabeth, Zachary, John the Baptist, Joseph and especially Mary who are seized and filled with the Holy Breath. This is in some way the first Pentecost. At the second descent it is the apostles who are filled with the Holy Breath and who receive power to cast out demons. Miracles characterize the public ministry of Jesus, in particular his transfiguration where the voice from on high comes from the "cloud" (Luke 9. 35) which is the sign of the Breath of God. Therefore the disciples would be guilty if they did not recognize this period in which God "breathes": "When you find a cloud rising out of the west, you say at once, There is rain coming, and so it does; when you find the south-west wind blowing, you say, It will be hot, and so it is. Poor fools, you know well enough how to interpret the face of the land and sky; can you not interpret the times you live in?" (Luke 12. 54–56).

Finally, a third influx of the Breath of God invaded the world at the moment when Jesus rose. This time it is as though the apostles received the Holy Breath for the first time inasmuch as they received him fully. Jesus revealed to them an understanding of the Scriptures and gave them confidence to speak to the nations, power to cast out demons and to work miracles in presenting the signs of salvation to the world. After the resurrection, this is Pentecost properly so called. In the radiance of the risen Christ, the Breath of God is then poured out upon the dry bones of this world which sin has put to death, and an immense body rises up all about, a body animated by one and the same breathing, that is, vivified by the same Breath (the Holy Breath of God), and this is the Church.

Christians have not yet fully explored this mysterious life-giving Breath—*Spiritum vivificantem*. The words of Jesus after the Last Supper and the promise of the Holy Breath gradually take on their full meaning when the fiery breath of the Most High comes down on the Cenacle. The apostles become conscious of the powers which had been given them, of the justice and holiness which the invasion by the Holy Breath brought with it, and in this way God prepares through his last inspired writer, St John, what will place the seal on this Revelation: the Holy Breath of God is not only "something", a breath which comes from God—a neuter word in Greek—but Someone.

THE THREEFOLD BEGINNING OF MESSIANIC TIMES

Elizabeth and Mary: the Messianic Dawn

Different are the stages of Revelation in which God makes clear, at times immediately, at others at a distance and sometimes at a great distance, the events wrought by his Providence, and often the realization of these events is different still. Concerning ourselves only with these latter we can see how the Breath of God is successively manifested from the birth of the Messias until his glorification at the right hand of the Father.

The first persons to be touched by the Breath of the Holy Spirit, during the period in which the Messias came, are Zachary and Elizabeth, the future parents of John the Baptist. Everything still seems to take place in an Old Testament atmosphere. Although "just" and "irreproachable" (Luke 1. 6), they had no child, which was not particularly a sign of God's blessing (cf. Gen. 1. 28; 9. 1; 27. 27, etc.). "Elizabeth was barren, and both were now well advanced in years" (Luke 1. 7). It is almost to the letter the history of Abraham and Sara (Gen. 18. 11), of Manue and his wife (Judges 13. 3) and Elcana and Anna (1 Kings 1. 1–8). Every woman considered her barrenness a curse, an irremedial misfortune, even though she was greatly loved by her husband. This was the case, in particular, with the wife of Elcana who, to console her because of her tears, said to her: "Is it not worth the love of ten sons, the love I bear you?" (1 Kings 1. 8). But these three women, like Elizabeth, were also loved by God, and God "blessed" them. Be assured, Zachary, the angel of the Lord said to him, "thy wife is to bear thee a son to whom thou shalt give the name John. Joy and gladness shall be thine and many hearts shall rejoice over his birth, for he is to be high in the Lord's favour; he is to drink neither wine nor strong drink; and from the time when he is yet a child in his mother's womb he shall be filled with the Holy Spirit. He shall bring back many of the sons of Israel to the Lord their God, ushering in his advent in the spirit and power of an Elias" (Luke 1. 13–17).

We are in the full "wind of God". In just a few lines there is presented the manifold action of the Breath of God. It is he who gives life and grants fertility and life to barren wombs. It is he who gives the joy and gladness which the evangelist often mentions in this first descent of the Holy Breath at the inauguration of messianic times (cf. 1. 28, 46, 58; 2. 10, etc.). He it is who has filled the prophets, of whom Elias is the type, the Elias who was carried off to heaven by this same Breath. There is a special share in the Breath and the power of God which the "Nazarites" receive—such as Samson, the son of Manue, or Samuel, the son of Elcana and Anna—those who were promised to God (either by themselves or by their mother) and who especially undertook to drink "neither wine nor strong drink". But John will be reached in a very special way by the Breath of God, he will be "filled" with it, and that "in his mother's womb", that is to say, not in a transitory manner, for an instant, but in a stable and permanent manner. The child will not be like others. While he "was growing" and "his spirit was achieving strength" (Luke 1. 80), the Breath of God drew him into the desert, where the people of God were formed, until he "was manifest to Israel" (id.). And finally, one last observation, the Breath which fills the child is the sanctifying

Spirit, who not only sanctifies him but bestows upon him the power to "bring back many of the sons of Israel to the Lord their God", to unite as well "the hearts of all, the fathers with the children and teach the disobedient the wisdom that makes men just" (Luke 1. 16–17; cf. 1. 69).

It is this same gust of supernatural wind which before long acts on Mary. The relation between these two actions is rightly stressed by St Luke (1. 36): the angel says again to her, "Rejoice", thereby recalling the messianic prophecy of Zacharias:

> Glad news for thee, widowed Sion;
> Cry out for happiness, Jerusalem forlorn!
> See where thy king comes to greet thee.
>
> (Zach. 9. 9.)

The whole angelic message is inspired by messianic prophecies.

But how will Mary be a mother since she promised to "have no knowledge of man" (Luke 1. 34)? "The Holy Spirit will come upon thee, and the power of the most High will overshadow thee" (1. 35): an expression which, in the Old Testament, denotes the shining cloud, the sign of Yahweh's breath. The Breath of God rests upon Mary in order to make her fruitful, just as it rested upon the primordial waters in the beginning (Gen. 1. 1). It is to her that the prophet referred when he cried out: "Maid shall be with child, and shall bear a son that shall be called Emmanuel" (Isaias 7. 14).

And just as Elizabeth "was filled with the Holy Spirit" at the approach of Mary and prophesied, crying out with a loud voice: "Blessed art thou among women and blessed is the fruit of thy womb" (Luke 1. 41–2), so Mary prophesied in singing a canticle replete with allusions from the canticle of Anna (1 Kings 2. 1–10), from a prophecy of Isaias (29. 19) and mainly from the Psalms. Both are conscious of having been seized by the great wind of God, of being taken into his Breath, even if they are not yet fully aware who this child is, what he shall be and do, and of the Person who does this "breathing", the Holy

Spirit. When a strong wind blows that can carry us with it, no one knows whence it comes or whither it leads.

Other persons with Elizabeth and Mary were seized by the Breath of God and made witnesses of this messianic dawn. Such are Zachary, Simeon awaiting the preferment of Israel (Luke 2. 25) and the prophetess Anna, daughter of Phanuel. All these prophesy. They all see in this child the awaited Messias, the "Christ whom the Lord has anointed" (Luke 2. 26), the Liberator looked for by "all that patiently waited for the deliverance of Israel" (Luke 2. 38).

And John the Baptist, when the time came for his preaching, never tired repeating: "As for me, I am baptizing (immersing) you with water, for your repentance; but one is to come after me who is mightier than I . . .; he will baptize (immerse) you with the Holy Ghost and with fire" (Matt. 3. 11; cf. Mark 1. 8; Luke 3. 16; John 1. 33), which describes the essential task of the Messias who is to regenerate humanity in the Holy Breath.

Fire, we saw, is intimately associated with certain manifestations of God. "In the midst of fire" (Deut. 4. 12) Yahweh manifested himself on Horeb in Sinai (Exod. 19, 18), in the burning bush (Exod. 3. 2), in the covenant (Gen. 15. 17). Yahweh himself is a "fire that consumes" (Deut. 4. 24; 9. 3; Exod. 24. 17). So also is his Breath. Jesus said: "It is fire that I have come to spread over the earth" (Luke 12. 49).

The baptism of Jesus: solemn consecration of the Messias

Jesus' baptism was the occasion for a new "Pentecostal" wind, a foreshadowing of abundant rain and heavenly blessings.

Like most of the events in Jesus' life, his baptism in the Jordan takes on its full meaning only when we set it against its background of prefigurative situations and actions in the Old Testament. The allusions of the evangelists and their descriptions of the scene make us think of the creation account, of the Exodus, of Isaias' messianic prayer (63–64) and of the way in which they already interpreted the Song of Songs at the time of Christ.

The "descent of the Spirit" (we now use both terms, Spirit or Breath, to direct the reader towards the Reality which neither of these terms used separately can fully express) calls to mind, first of all, the descent of the Holy Breath upon the primordial waters (Gen. 1. 2) and suggests a new creation or regeneration. The liturgy for the blessing of the font on Easter night has blended these two events, the creation and sanctification of the waters of the Jordan, in a beautiful preface which begins: "Lord God, whose Spirit hovered over the waters in the beginning so that the nature of water already contains in germ the power of sanctifying souls. . .". In commenting on the baptism of Jesus Fr Lagrange writes: "Just as the Holy Spirit hovered over the primordial water like a dove, so the Spirit descends in the form of a dove before Jesus has left the waters; the Holy Spirit will act in the same way upon the waters to give them a supernatural power."[2] Thus "at the very moment when Jesus submits himself to the baptism of water by the precursor, he transforms it into baptism in the Holy Spirit who will give birth to the messianic community".[3] The association of water and the Holy Spirit was traditional, as we have seen, at least since Ezechiel (36. 25–27; cf. also Isaias 44. 3–5; Psalm 50. 9, 18).

But the descent of the Spirit as a bird which "hovers" (this verb is used in Gen. 1. 2) brings to mind also the Canticle of Moses (Deut. 32. 1–43) in the desert. Moses gives thanks to God for his power and blessings; he recalls the primitive chaos in the desert out of which Israel was formed and he sings: "so the eagle that would incite its young to venture in the air now hovers about them, now spreads its wings and takes them up to rest on its own shoulders" (Deut. 32. 11).

Matthew's account of Jesus' baptism calls to mind the events of the Exodus, particularly as Isaias relates them in his great eschatological prayer (63–64): just as the people of Israel was

[2] *Evangile selon Saint Marc*, Paris, 1942, page 13.

[3] A. Feuillet, "Le symbolisme de la colombe dans les récits évangéliques" in *Recherches de Science Religieuse* (Oct.–Dec. 1958, pp. 524–44), p. 530. This excellent study has been of considerable use here.

guided by the Spirit of Yahweh into the desert after the passage through the Red Sea (Isaias 63. 14), so Jesus was led into the desert after his baptism in the Jordan. Isaias cried out in a transport of hope: "Wouldst thou but part asunder and come down" (Isaias 64. 1), and now, for Jesus, "suddenly heaven was opened" (Matt. 3. 16).

We are no longer concerned with the new creation but with the messianic realization. The divine promises foretold by the prophets are in the course of being fulfilled. But that is not all.

What does the dove which descends upon Jesus represent? Undoubtedly, the "Holy Spirit", as Mark explicitly says, but also something else. Just as the tongues of fire at Pentecost symbolize the Spirit as well as that fruit of the Spirit represented by the gift of tongues to the apostles, and which is essentially the gathering together, through the Holy Spirit and the Word of the apostles, of the scattered peoples whose languages, under the symbol of Babel, are no longer mutually understood, so here the dove designates essentially Israel, "the perfect community in the era of grace",[4] constituted by the sudden entry of the Holy Spirit.

Indeed, for Osee, the dove is the people of Israel returning from exile, purified at last: "Fluttering like sparrow or dove from Egypt, from the Assyrian country, and in their own home, the Lord says, I will give them rest" (Osee 11. 11; cf. 7. 11). For the psalmist too, the dove is the people loved by God: "Wilt thou throw to wild beasts, thy dove?" (Psalm 73. 19).

It is the people which "as a dove with silvered wings" settles in Canaan (Psalm 67. 14). But for the Jews in the time of Christ it is especially the people of Israel, referred to as a dove in the Song of Songs. The phrase: "my dove, my perfect one" (Song of Songs 2. 14; 5. 2; 6. 9 and also 1. 15; 4. 1; 5. 12) describes "the spouse of Yahweh in the state which is to be its own once the covenant is restored, and it refers to the longing for the new Exodus announced by the prophets".[5] Thus John, who baptized

[4] A. Feuillet, *art. cit.*, p. 538.
[5] Id., p. 535.

Jesus and saw the dove, symbol of the spouse, can cry out:
"The bride is for the bridegroom" (John 3. 29). He adds that
"the bridegroom's friend who stands by and listens to him,
rejoices too, rejoices at hearing the bridegroom's voice; and
this joy is mine now in full measure". These words bring to
mind also the cry of joy from the spouse in the Song of Songs
when she hears "the voice of her true love" (2. 8, 10, 14; 5. 2).
All that John the Baptist discovers about Jesus, he discovers
during the baptismal scene. It is there that he recognizes God's
Chosen One (John 1. 34), the Lamb of God (1. 29), the Spouse,
the substitute for Israel, the messianic king.

The dove, symbol of the Holy Spirit and the Church, announces the intimate relationship which exists between the
Holy Spirit and the Church. It is in fact the Holy Spirit who
gathers together the scattered peoples into one Church. In the
third part of the Apostles' Creed, which was originally a profession of faith at baptism, the catechumen, after having pro-
fessed his faith in the Father: "I believe in God, the Father
almighty", and then his faith in Christ: "I believe in Jesus
Christ, his only Son . . .", proclaims his faith in the Holy
Spirit, saying: "I believe in the Holy Spirit, the Holy Catholic
Church". The Holy Spirit is the one who forms the Church,
constitutes it, organizes it and vivifies it unceasingly. That is
why faith in the Holy Spirit is always linked with the Church.
That is why the Spirit is joined to the Church in prayer, to express the impatient longing for the definitive encounter with
Christ: "The Spirit and the bride say: Come!" (Apoc. 22. 17).
That is why the Holy Spirit is always present in the sacramental
liturgy of the Church, assists her, gives value to her actions.
This very special assistance bears the special name *epiclesis* in
the offering and consecration of the eucharistic oblations. Does
not St John give us an insight into this intimate relationship
of the Spirit with the Church when he describes in his Gospel
what the Precursor saw: "The Spirit coming down from
heaven like a dove" (1. 32), while he himself, in his Apocalypse,
saw through a similar opening in the heavens, the "heavenly

Jerusalem" (Gal. 4. 26), which is free, the Church, "being sent down from heaven by God, all clothed in readiness, like a bride, who has adorned herself to meet her husband" (Apoc. 21. 2)? The liturgy has made the baptism of Christ the feast of his wedding with the Church in spontaneously considering together the mystery of the nuptials at the Jordan, the mystery of the Magi and the mystery of Cana: "Today, the Church has been united to the heavenly spouse for Christ has washed her sins in the Jordan. The Magi hasten with gifts to the royal nuptials and the water, changed into wine, rejoices the wedding-guests, Alleluia."[6]

Thus the symbol of the dove in relation to the water of the river, the opening in the heavens, the voice coming from heaven, signifies a descent of divine benefits and especially the most precious of all, the Holy Spirit. The prophecy of Isaias (63–64) is realized. Jesus, the new Moses, the head and representative of the new Israel, invested with all the divine favours, inaugurates, this time solemnly, messianic times.

Immediately afterwards, "sent into the desert by the Spirit" (Mark 1. 12), like Moses after the passage through the Red Sea, Jesus goes to be tempted, that is, he goes to undergo in himself and in reference to his mission, considered in some sort as Israel's substitute, "the trials encountered by the Hebrews in their crossing of the Sinai desert".[7]

During the following three years the public life of Jesus continues in the effulgence of this baptismal theophany, that is, the influence of the Spirit who descended upon him visibly does not cease to be manifested. The outstanding events of this manifestation are, up to the resurrection, the transfiguration and all the miracles of Jesus, his struggle against the evil "spirits" and his prophetic utterances.

The transfiguration is above all a prophetic sign which, in certain respects, recalls the baptism. In both the Father presents his Son. But the baptism inaugurates Jesus' messianic

[6] Antiphon for the feast of the Epiphany.
[7] A. Feuillet, art. cit., p. 544.

rôle, manifests his investiture as Messias; the transfiguration shows the glory to come, that of his coming in the future (Luke 9. 26) after the Passion. At the baptism the Holy Spirit is present under the unusual form of a dove; at the transfiguration he is present under the sign of the shining cloud, similar to that which pointed out the way for the Hebrews when they left Egypt, similar also to all those clouds in which Yahweh manifested his presence or glory (Exod. 13. 22; 19. 9, 16; 24. 15, 16; Deut. 4. 11; 2 Kings 8. 10, 12; Ps. 17. 12; 24. 15, 16), and finally like that "shadow" which was over Mary when she conceived by the Holy Spirit (compare Luke 1. 35 and 9. 34). Likewise it is upon the clouds of heaven that Jesus will appear at his return (Matt. 24. 30; cf. Dan. 7. 13; Apoc. 1. 7).

At his baptism, John the Baptist sees and understands that Jesus is the Chosen of God; at the transfiguration Jesus has three witnesses, the same who accompanied him when he raised up the daughter of Jairus (Mark 5. 37), the same, also, who were to be the privileged witnesses of his agony (Mark 14. 33).

At his baptism, Jesus appears only in his "earthly" body; at the transfiguration he manifests his "heavenly" body, that body which the Spirit of God will one day give to all those who will be reunited through him (cf. 1 Cor. 15. 44–50). At the baptism all is inaugurated and there is no immediate need of fear: the Voice is alone; at the transfiguration the apostles begin to understand the prophecy of the Passion and are afraid: Moses and Elias, the Law and the Prophets, the most representative persons of the Old Testament, testify that he is indeed the chosen One for whom Israel was waiting; the Spirit of God here revives their faith.

Clearly, from his baptism to his resurrection the life of Jesus is under the sign of the Holy Breath. He is the Messias, invested with the Breath of God, completely filled and radiant, through his Word and his miracles, with the Breath, having just inaugurated the Kingdom of God through the Gift of the Breath.

Now, the great sin is "the sin against the Breath of the Holy

Spirit". "There is no one who speaks a word against the Son
of Man but may find forgiveness; there will be no forgiveness
for the man who blasphemes against the Holy Spirit" (Luke
12. 10; cf. Matt. 12. 32). "Believe me, there is pardon for all
the other sins of mankind and the blasphemies they utter; but
if a man blasphemes against the Holy Spirit, there is no pardon
for him in all eternity" (Mark 3. 28–9). A fearful saying.
Everyone can err and fail, but he who has been seized by the
Spirit of God, who finds himself caught up in the vivifying
breath and who is face to face with a manifestly divine work,
miracle, deed or word on the part of Christ, cannot deny that
God is there without sinning gravely. St Paul said: "Do not
distress God's Holy Spirit" (Ephes. 4. 30). Indeed, the man who
is distressed and therefore sad, withdraws within himself in
abandoning him who has distressed him.

So we must ask God untiringly for his Holy Breath (Luke 13.
13) and without distrusting our own breath: "Blessed are the
poor in spirit" (Matt. 5. 3), those who have a feeble breath,
which refers metaphorically to the little ones, the humble.
Indeed, God "revives the breath of the humble" (cf. Isaias
57. 15).

Above all, we must be on our guard and struggle. The Breath
of God can truly reign only if it has first of all conquered the
adverse breaths, that is to say the bad angels or "demons", to
use the term borrowed from Hellenism. We call them "spirits"
or "breaths" because they are immaterial (cf. Luke 24. 37–9),
and also because, in spite of their malice, they derive their life
or more precisely their breath (of life) from God. We have
already seen how God commanded the evil spirits in the Old
Testament (cf. Judges 9. 23–4; 1 Kings 16. 14–23; 19. 9; 2
Kings 22. 22, etc.). The angels possess a certain divine power,
but the bad ones use it for evil. It is they who are responsible
for the diseases and weaknesses as well as the vices and evil
inclinations of men, and so much so that diseases and vices
will be named after demons. The ancient anthropology of the
Fathers of the Church retained this way of looking at things

and ascribed the humours as well as the passions, qualities or shortcomings of men to certain angels.

Jesus began his public life under the sign of a defeat for Satan, the Tempter, who "departed from him" (Luke 4. 13) after having tried in vain. But St Luke adds "departing from him, he left him in peace until the time should come" (Luke 4. 13). And as he departed, "angels came and ministered to him" (Matt. 4. 11). Jesus is master of the spirits as Yahweh was master of the winds, the breaths, of all life and all holiness. On one occasion Jesus orders the evil spirits in such a way that everyone is in awe of him: "Wonder fell upon them all, as they said to one another, What is this word of his? See how he has authority and power to lay his command on the unclean spirits, so that they come out!" (Luke 4. 36). On another occasion he simply heals by a power that goes forth from him (Luke 6. 19; 8. 46). His power consists in freeing "from evil spirits and from sicknesses" (Luke 8. 2) as well as driving out demons on the way (Matt. 8. 28) or forgiving sins (Luke 5. 20). There is a cosmic duel between him and the powers of darkness until the devil is vanquished, and that helps us experience in advance both the acuteness of the struggle which is let loose in the heart of man when "the evil one comes and carries off what was sown in his heart" (Matt. 13. 19) and the power of the Spirit of God which Christ will give us as a gift.

This force of the Breath in and through which he acts does not leave Jesus humanly indifferent. On many occasions the Gospel draws our attention to the effects of the Holy Breath in his humanity. When the disciples return rejoicing from their apostolic errand, Jesus "was filled with gladness by the Spirit" (Luke 10. 21). When Mary, the sister of Lazarus, throws herself at the feet of Jesus and weeps over the death of her brother, Jesus "sighed deeply" (John 11. 33). Finally, at the Last Supper, Jesus knowing he was to be betrayed, "was troubled in spirit" (John 13. 21, Douay Version). In this gigantic conflict where the Master of Life and the emperor of Death meet each other, the flesh cannot remain serene and without emotion when the spirit of man keeps watch, attacks and defends itself. In Jesus, as later in his disciples, the whole being of man is mobilized.

But victory will come; Jesus prophetically sees "Satan cast down like a lightning flash from heaven" (Luke 10. 18), and the disciples can have confidence: they have received "the right to trample on snakes and scorpions, and all the powers of the enemy" (Luke 10. 19). But the important thing is not to subject spirits but to have their name written in heaven (Luke 10. 20). It is in view of this glory that Jesus promises his disciples that they will soon be "baptized in the Spirit", that is, be "immersed in the Holy Breath" (Acts 1. 5 and cf. John 1. 34), and that they will receive a new strength, that of the Holy Breath who will come down upon them (cf. Acts 1. 8).

St John contemplated Jesus' last breath: "He bowed his head and yielded up his spirit" (John 19. 30). This last breath "serves as a prelude to the outpouring of the Spirit"[8] upon the apostles and disciples when Jesus has been glorified. At this moment, even before the solemn descent of the Holy Breath upon the apostles, he himself "breathed upon them and said to them, Receive the Holy Spirit" (John 20. 22). The Twelve are henceforth the ἀπόστολοι διὰ Πνεύματος ʽΑγίου, Apostles by virtue of the Holy Breath (Acts 1. 2).

Pentecost, the solemn diffusion of the messianic breath

From "breath" to "breath", to the immaterial "breath" which is the spirit; from the "breath of Yahweh's mouth" which enabled the Hebrews to cross the Red Sea and leave Egypt, to the Holy Breath which led Jesus into the desert and through him performed all sorts of miracles and signs, this is how the Holy Spirit gradually manifests himself and leads the children of God. It is no longer simply a cosmic force, although directly attributed to God, no longer only the breath lent to the living things in the whole of creation, it is a power of holiness. The life which it can give and is going to give is a divine life. As the revelation of the Holy Breath becomes more

[8] *Bible de Jérusalem*, p. 1,427, note g.

precise, the distance which, in relation to our understanding of it, was still separating it from God, vanishes. It is God who guides history, who sanctifies and deifies us.

The pagans were fully able to imagine gods whose "breath" is revealed in the wind or in the life and health of living beings, but such breaths, even though attributed to the gods, do not transcend what we can see in nature. The pagan religions remain naturalistic. God is not revealed in them as an autonomous personality, free as regards the course of nature. The God of Israel, on the contrary, guides history. The winds or breaths which he sends have a direction or meaning towards which the people led by God gradually advances. They have, beyond their nature, a meaning that is transcendent. The Breath of Yahweh is, like the Ark, the permanent presence of Yahweh in the midst of his people; like the column of cloud, it is a sign, a direction and a light from God; like the strong hand or the arm of God which saves his people from the greatest perils (cf. Isaias 63. 9–14, and Nehemias 9. 20), like the very Face of God (Psalm 50. 12–14)—God himself.

The Breath of God sends and sustains the words of the prophets, makes the word of the Law heard and places it in the heart (cf. Deut. 30. 11–14). Soon all will be "prophets", all will be animated with the Breath which makes them understand what God says and cling to his Word. The Breath will be "for ever" with Christians (John 14. 16). He is the object of the Promise, the sign and reality of the new and eternal covenant (Jer. 31. 33; Ezech. 36. 27; Heb. 9. 14–15). That is why he will be given through the anointing with oil (2 Cor. 1. 21–2), whose property consists in imbuing what it touches in a permanent manner. Christ himself is the Anointed One *par excellence* because he is completely filled with the Breath of God: "The Spirit of the Lord is upon me, he has anointed me" (Luke 4. 18).

The gift of the Holy Breath which crowns the execution of God's plans is, therefore, also the term of Christ's work. At Pentecost, he is poured out and given to the apostles and with them to the Church. He constitutes "a pledge of the inheritance which is ours, to redeem it for us and bring us into possession of it, and so manifest God's glory" (Ephes. 1. 14; cf. 2 Cor. 1. 21–2).

The gift of the Holy Breath is a sign that a new world is born, a world in which God has come to take up his abode and live among men. "When the fullness of time was come", says St Paul to the Galatians, "God sent his Son, made of a woman, made under the law, that we might receive the adoption of sons" (Gal. 4. 5, Douay Version). The adoption of sons is the special work of the Holy Breath: "Those who follow the leading of God's Spirit are all God's sons; the spirit you have now received is not, as of old, a spirit of slavery to govern you by fear, it is the spirit of adoption which makes us cry out, Abba, Father. The Spirit himself thus assures our spirit that we are children of God; and if we are children of God, then we are his heirs too; heirs of God, sharing the inheritance of Christ" (Rom. 8. 14–17; cf. Gal. 4. 6).

To be sure, the Holy Breath was manifested many times; first of all at the creation, then in the time of Moses, among the prophets and wise men of Israel, and finally at the moment of Jesus' conception and his birth, at the moment of his baptism and during his ministry. But all these manifestations of particular gifts to individuals on special occasions or for particular missions merely foreshadowed a more solemn manifestation of a more generous, universal and, this time, definite gift.

Not only a more generous gift but also a gift that brings a renewal. The Breath of God did indeed bring to Moses the "Word" of God and communicate to him the divine law, but this same law was the reason for the condemnation of certain pharisees who glorified in it. The "rule of the law" as such will be surpassed. Woe to those who trust in themselves or in their deeds. Only the Breath of God, that is, his Power and Life, can save us. It is not mere "observance of the law" that brings him to us: St Paul makes this point to the Galatians in a very vivid manner: "Was it from the observance of the law that the Spirit came to you?" (Gal. 3. 2).

Many expressions in the Old Testament which are very often misunderstood, such as the "Law", the "flesh", the "letter", are to be understood in this sense: salvation is not to be found in man's strength but in the Power of God communicated in his Breath. "Only the spirit gives life, the flesh is of no avail" (John 6. 63). This does not mean that it is necessary to reject all that is external and retain only the inner and "spiritual" interpretation of Jesus' teaching, which would mean that the "flesh" (that is man left to himself) does not have the power to perform a salutary act; it is the Breath, the Power of God that gives life. "God is a spirit, and those who worship him must worship him in spirit and in truth" (John 4. 24): nor do these words signify that we must adore him in the inner sanctuary of our "spirit" or "our religious needs" but "on the contrary, we must renounce all attempts at solitary worship, all efforts to draw near to God by our own strivings".[9] The Pauline opposition between "the letter that kills" and "the Breath that gives life" (cf. 2 Cor. 3. 6) is to be understood in the same sense: all human sufficiency, appealing to the Law, is deadly for man; only the Breath of God gives the believer the power not to falter in the execution of the law and to accomplish it perfectly and freely.

The gift of the Breath is gratuitous. Christ merits it and bestows it on us through his passion and his resurrection (cf. John 7. 39). And he gives it to those who believe in him. The apostles, in bearing the Word which gives the Holy Breath to those who "listen to it", can truly be called "God's assistants" (cf. 1 Cor. 3. 9).

This generous and universal gift of the Breath after the glorification of Christ is such a novelty that St Paul was able to compare the two systems: that of the Law which at last, as regards man, is seen as a regime of condemnation and death, and that of the Holy Breath which alone bestows and guarantees life:

[9] Jacques Guillet, *Thèmes Bibliques*, coll. Théologie (Paris, Aubier, 1951), p. 223.

All our ability comes from God, since it is he who has enabled
us to promulgate his new law to men. It is a spiritual, not a written
law; the written law inflicts death, whereas the spiritual law
brings life. We know how that sentence of death, engraved in
writing upon stone, was promulgated to men in a dazzling cloud,
so that the people of Israel could not look Moses in the face for
the brightness of it [Exod. 34. 35], although that brightness soon
passed away. How much more dazzling, then, must be the brightness in which the spiritual law is promulgated to them! If there
is a splendour in the proclamation of our guilt, there must be
more splendour yet in the proclamation of our acquittal. (2 Cor.
3. 5–9.)

THE MEMORY AND REFLECTION INSPIRED BY JOHN

John's Gospel dates from the end of the first century. It is the
last of the New Testament writings or rather next to the last if
the first epistle of the beloved Apostle is later. John witnessed
the development of the Judaeo-Christian communities in
Jerusalem and its environs, as well as the development of the
hellenistic Christians whose origin and centre was at Antioch.
He was familiar with the exploits of the procurators Felix,
Festus, Albinus and Florus; he was aware of the persecutions
ordered by Nero, the expeditions of Vespasian and Titus in
Palestine and the sufferings at Jerusalem, in turn captured and
recaptured before the final Roman victory.

All these events clarified in a single day the age old "hope"
which the Jews placed in their Messias and brought the words
and teaching of Jesus into great prominence. John strengthened
the courage of the Christians, probably during the persecution
of Domitian, by writing his Apocalypse. The saying of Jesus,
"Take courage, I have overcome the world" (John 16. 33), is
always true.

It is in the light of these events, seen in his thoughts in relation to the words and passion of Jesus, that John continued his
meditation, itself sustained, made fruitful and inspired by the

Holy Breath, and that, at the end of his life, he wrote his Gospel. The events are the same, but the Holy Breath given by Jesus "will in his turn make everything plain and recall to your minds everything I have said to you" (John 14. 26). "It will be for him . . . to guide you into all truth" (John 16. 13). God acts in time, slowly and patiently. It is not surprising then that John's Gospel forms for us an additional revelation to the "synoptics".

John does not relate the scene of Jesus' baptism which we saw was the inaugural manifestation of the kingdom of the Messias and his investiture; but he does tell us of the testimony of the Precursor after the baptism. Seeing Jesus coming to him, John the Baptist remembering "the Spirit coming down from heaven like a dove and resting upon him" (John 1. 32) declares: "This is the Son of God," and "Look, this is the Lamb of God" (John 1. 34, 29), that is, Look, the "Servant" of Yahweh, prophesied by Isaias (53), who bears the sins of men and offers himself as an expiatory lamb (Lev. 14), and at the same time the new paschal Lamb (Exod. 12. 1 and John 19. 36), symbol of Israel's redemption (cf. Acts 8. 31–5; 1 Cor. 5. 7; 1 Peter 1. 18–20). This solemn manifestation of the Holy Breath opened the eyes of John the Baptist and made him immediately recognize who Jesus was.

Jesus is he who comes from on high and who, by reason of this origin, brings us salvation. No man "without being born from above" (John 3. 3), that is, "unless birth comes to him from water and from the Holy Spirit, can enter into the kingdom of heaven" (John 3. 5). The relation between the Breath and water, traditional at least since Ezechiel (39. 29) and Isaias (44. 3), here announces salvation by baptism, immersion in the Breath, or at least in water imbued with the virtue of the Breath. "What is born by natural birth is a thing of nature, what is born by spiritual birth is a thing of spirit. Do not be surprised then at my telling thee, You must be born anew" (John 3. 7). The opposition which we observe from the beginning between the flesh and the breath, here takes on its strongest

and definitive meaning, that which explains the whole movement of revelation until this day. What is born of man is merely
human. What is born of the Breath, of the life of God, is divine.
But the Breath here is no longer only the power of natural life
or of wonders, miracles or prophecy; it is essentially the power
of holiness, sanctification, of life in God and with God, the
power of renewal for the whole being and not only, needless to
say, for the "spirit". He it is who will raise up our bodies if he
dwells in us, just as he raised up Jesus from among the dead
(Rom. 8. 11).

John comes back repeatedly to this necessary and fundamental action of the Breath. We meet it under the symbol of
living water in the encounter with the Samaritan woman (John
4. 11), and in the encounter on the feast of Tabernacles (John
7. 37–9). In the Book of Consolation, the theme of water,
associated with the Breath, enriches the new image. Not only
does the Breath of God bring water through rain, but transforms the barren earth and gives it power to conceive new
springs and streams (Isaias 44. 3). In the same way, "from
Jesus' bosom" (cf. John 7. 38) or perhaps according to other
versions, "from the bosom of him who believes", "fountains of
living water shall flow" (John 7. 38). And John explains: "He
was speaking here of the Spirit which was to be received by
those who learned to believe in him; the Spirit which has not
yet been given to men, because Jesus has not yet been raised to
glory" (John 7. 39). When Jesus imparted the Breath to his
Church, then the whole Church was assisted by him and
walked in the power of the Breath.

The Discourse after the Last Supper

Without further delay we come to the Discourse after the
Last Supper which, for St John, is central in the revelation of
the Holy Breath.

What is new in this Discourse is that the Holy Breath is presented to us under a name which is that of a Person: the "Paraclete". Now, in his first Epistle St John gives this name to Christ

himself: "If any of us does fall into sin, we have an advocate (Paraclete) to plead our cause before the Father in the Just One, Jesus Christ" (1 John 2. 1). In this same discourse the Holy Breath is presented as "another" Paraclete (John 14. 16). At one and the same time this common appellation makes us think that we are concerned with two similar persons. What, then, is a paraclete?

Paraclete, in Greek παράκλητος, comes from the verb παρακαλέω which means to call to one, to call for asking advice, to call to one's aid or defence, to invite, to appeal to. The Paraclete is one whom we call to our aid, and so, consequently, an advocate, a protector, an intercessor. The Greek παράκλησις means mainstay, assistance, defence, support or even exhortation, excitation. The translators of the New Testament sometimes render παράκλησις by Consolation. Hence παράκλητος becomes Consoler which is in fact one of the traditional names for the Holy Spirit. But we should remember that "consolation" did not always have the meaning we give it in our day: an alleviation of grief, pain or bitterness. Consoler did not always designate one who comforts persons in distress. In the Middle Ages the consoler is still one who gives courage to the despondent, who gives energy and courage to the weary. He is an animator, a support, a defender. The word is more suitable for the Holy Spirit in this particular sense. Nevertheless, St Jerome preferred not to translate παράκλητος; he has simply transcribed the Greek word into Latin: *Paracletus*. Many English translators imitated this and so we speak of the Paraclete. Perhaps that is more suitable owing to the fact that our "advocate", "defender", "consoler" is a unique advocate. He has no equal. Indeed, Jesus said to his apostles: the Paraclete will be "with you for ever" (John 14. 17), "he will be continually at your side, nay, he will be in you" (14. 17), "he will make everything plain and recall to your minds everything I have said to you" (14. 26), "to guide you into all truth . . . and he will make plain to you what is still to come" (16. 13).

In the great cosmic process which is unfolding before God

until the final day between Satan and the "woman", the spouse of Christ who is the Church and whom St John sees prophetically in his Apocalypse (12), Satan is presented as the "accuser of our brethren . . . day and night he stood accusing them in God's presence" (12. 10). The Paraclete, on the other hand, is our advocate, our defender. He defends those whom Satan accuses.

But Satan does not only denounce nor the Paraclete only plead. Satan is the spirit of disorder (1 John 4. 6), the spirit of falsehood and murder (John 8. 44), opposed to the spirit of truth (1 John 5. 6). The Holy Breath who here reveals under the name of Paraclete an aspect of his personality, is defender and witness of a cause slandered by the devil, but he is a defender and a witness entirely within those in whose favour he bears witness. In them, as in all those who have received him, "the Spirit himself thus assures our spirit that we are children of God" (Rom. 8. 16) and thus liberated from the hold of the devil, the accuser. When the disciples "will be brought before governors and kings" (Matt. 10. 18) because of Christ, they will not have to fear: "words will be given you when the time comes", Jesus says to them; "it is not you who speak, it is the Spirit of your Father that speaks in you" (Matt. 10. 19–20; cf. John 15. 26–7). Filled with the Holy Spirit, the apostles will always be able to bear witness to Jesus. The Holy Breath "will come", said Jesus, "and it will be for him to prove the world wrong, about sin, and about rightness of heart and about judging" (John 16. 8). The Paraclete will bring to full light the *sin* of the world which is its incredulity (John 16. 9); he will manifest the perfect justice of the cause of Christ, of him who will show his heavenly origin and his divine sonship by going back to heaven (John 16. 10); he will be the sign of the judgement according to which the death of Jesus signifies the condemnation of the Prince of this world (John 16. 11). The Paraclete is indeed advocate, defender, assessor, but in this invisible combat in which the disciple of Christ engages with Satan, he is in the very heart of the one he defends, assists, counsels. He is his inner force, energy, dynamism, which at each moment restores him and renews his youth.

To complete the divine portrait which we are trying to sketch, it is not unprofitable to compare the two words *Paraclete* and *Church*. They have in fact the same etymology. Both come from *caleo* (in Latin, *vocare*). The Church is the *convocation* of all believers, assisted by him who is not only her *Advocate* before the Father, who defends her rights, but above all who creates her justice, the One who gives her her holiness, her inner strength, who is her Breath of life, one Breath for all the members, and establishes her in unity.

The Discourse after the Last Supper, slowly assimilated by St John during the trying years of his solitude, crowns in some sort the revelation of the Holy Breath. In truth, without what precedes it we should not know a great deal about the personality of this Paraclete whom Christ announces to us. But without this Discourse, we should undoubtedly not know, or at all events know inadequately, that his Holy Breath whose action we have recognized throughout biblical history is "another Paraclete", a person like the Son.

The Messias, the Anointed One *par excellence*, came to communicate the Holy Breath to the *Convocation* of those who have been called by him and believe in him. He is gone, but he is replaced by this "other Paraclete" whom the Father "gives" (John 14. 16), or "sends in his name" (14. 26), or whom he himself "sends from the Father" (cf. 15. 26). In crowning the salvific plan of God, the Paraclete completes the work of Christ, he makes clear how Jesus fulfilled the Scriptures (5. 39), the meaning of his words and acts (14. 26; 16. 13; 1 John 2. 20 ff). He leads towards the whole truth (16. 13). To accept being lead by his Breath is to "enter into Life" (Matt. 18. 8–9).

CHAPTER V

HOW FAR CAN WE KNOW THE HOLY SPIRIT?

What was the faith of those who heard and accepted the message of the apostles after Pentecost? Or at least, since faith which is the gift of God and adherence to his ineffable truth, is always substantially the same, how did they make their belief explicit? How did they formulate it? And in particular, how did they use such terms as Holy Breath, Breath of Truth, the Spirit, the Paraclete?

One thing is certain: they were familiar with these and certain other names from their reading of the Scriptures and the preaching of the apostles.

IMMATERIAL BREATH

This word "breath" as used for God in such expressions as Breath of Yahweh, Breath of God, Holy Breath, gradually, according to the understanding of the believers, acquired its more noble spiritual meaning. Yet, for the Hebrews, it was never something material as a gust of wind or some similar movement is for us who analyse the elements of nature chemically. For them the breath of life and the wind were something immaterial, supra-terrestrial, something superior to the "flesh", and thus easily lent themselves to represent the effect of a divine activity or the divine activity itself. However, the idea which they developed was originally very near that of the natural

religions in which the forces and activities of nature were attributed to the gods. But gradually this conception was purified,
until finally "Breath of God" became a recognized title for
God, analogous to the sacred name. It now had a spiritual
meaning like our own word "spirit", the English equivalent of
Ruah or the corresponding Greek *Pneuma*; it is this meaning
which we now use more generally. This word is so traditional
and sacred in our religious language that we could not dispense
with it. But we should recall that it is the translation of a word
which at one time had a different meaning and that it now
bears an assumed as well as intellectual meaning, pregnant
with the whole religious tradition of Israel. We should also
bear in mind the etymology of this word "spirit" which is found
in words like aspire, inspire, words which, even in our day, are
used with a physical as well as spiritual meaning.

SOMEONE

Another thing is certain: the first Christians heard the Spirit
of God spoken of as "Someone" acting in them and in the
midst of them, sanctifying and uniting them to one another.
Whatever "gifts" are received, whatever "services", whatever
"the manifestations of power" (1 Cor. 12. 4–6), they know that
it is everywhere "the same Spirit". Certain formulas in which
the Spirit is associated with the Father and the Son, and on an
equal footing with them, if we may use the phrase, were familar
to them. Such formulas are, for example, the baptismal formula
which is mentioned for the first time in Matt. 28. 19, or the
beautiful liturgical formula which brings to a close 2 Corinthians (13. 13). There are many others: Rom. 1. 4; 15. 16, 30;
1 Cor. 2. 10, 14; 6. 11, 14, 15; 12. 4–6; 2 Cor. 1. 21 ff; Gal. 4. 6;
Philipp. 2. 1; Ephes. 1. 3–14; 2. 18–22; 4. 4–6; Tim. 3. 5 ff; Heb.
9. 14; 1 Peter 1. 2; 3. 18; 1 John 4. 2; Apoc. 1. 4 ff; 22. 1;
Acts 10. 38; 20. 28; John 14. 16; 18. 23. So the Spirit is God
just as the Father is God and Christ is God. The Spirit acts just
as the Father and the Son act; the very work of our deification

(cf. 2 Peter 1. 4; Acts 19. 28) and our divine filiation, divine activities, are ascribed as the especial work of the Spirit (Rom. 8. 8–30; Gal. 4. 6).

THE THIRD?

However, there was still no mention of the Trinity. It is true that we find in the Clementine edition of the Vulgate the famous verse: "Thus we have a threefold warrant in heaven, the Father, the Son and the Holy Spirit, three who are yet one" (1 John 5. 7). Yet we know that this verse does not appear in the Latin Vulgate prior to the ninth century. Thus its Johannine authorship is at least doubtful. True, Clement VIII accepted it into his edition of the Vulgate, but is this sufficient for the Church to regard it as inspired? So far the Magisterium has made no pronouncement on the point.[1]

The number three and consequently the much later term "trinity" are not found among the inspired texts which are definitely canonical. St Basil says: "In giving us the formula, Father, Son and Holy Spirit, our Lord does not mention number. . . . But by these sacred names he has revealed to us the faith which saves. . . . The number which expresses how many subjects there are was unfolded by reflection."[2] In time this number compelled recognition. The first to use the word Trias (*Trinitas*) to describe the union of the thre divine persons in God was Theophilus of Antioch, the sixth bishop of Antioch, in the second century. The Cappadocian Fathers and others adopted the usage. And so it entered Christian literature during the period of the anti-Arian and anti-Pneumatomachian councils, viz., the Council of Nicaea (325) and the Council of Constantinople (381). That is why St Basil could add that those who make difficulties with everything "have abused", contrary to the faith, the silence of the Scriptures.

Yet the introduction of a number into the divine unity

---

[1] Cf. Denzinger, *Enchiridion Symbolorum*, n. 2198.
[2] *De Spiritu Sancto*, Chapter 13.

created difficulties. Clearly, God is not a whole, and the Father, Son and Spirit "parts". Nor is God the sum total of persons measured in some sort by a number. Each person is infinite and the grandeur of the three is identical. In a well-known dispute in the thirteenth century, St Thomas collected no less than twenty-seven difficulties on the subject.[3] After considering some of the opinions which were current in his day, he stated in reply:

> When speaking of God, it does not seem right to me to use the "one" and the "many" which pertain to the genus of quantity, but rather the "one" and the "many" which is identified with being the "multiple" which corresponds to this "one". For the "one" and the "many" place in God the realities indicated, but they add nothing to these realities except their own distinction and indivision, as was shown above. Therefore, we grant that in so far as the "one" and the "many" add something to these realities they ought to be understood negatively; but in so far as they include in their meaning the realities spoken of, they ought to be understood positively.[4]

In other words, God cannot be measured in terms of "continuous quantity", as if it were possible to count a certain number of realities in God. God is beyond all measurement. When we say that his essence or nature is one, the unity we attribute to him is not a numerical unity, as when we say the Cyclops has one eye. It is a unity which signifies nothing other than being, or at least the absolute indivisibility of the being in question. And when we say that there are three persons, we do not imply that they can be counted, as for instance three children of a family; we simply speak of their incommunicability and distinction. The Father is not the Son nor the Spirit, and the Spirit is neither the Father nor the Son.

All these distinctions have some value; they prevent us from compromising, through some error of language, the unity of God which is at the very heart of our faith. "Listen then, Israel,

---

[3] *De Potentia*, qu. 9, art. 7. Cf. *Summa Theol.* Ia, qu. 30, art. 3.
[4] *De Potentia*, qu. 9, art. 7, c. in fine.

there is no Lord but the Lord thy God" (Deut. 6. 4), says the
first phrase of the Jewish prayer, the Shema, which Jesus
quoted to the Scribes who questioned him on the first com-
mandment (Mark 12. 29). During the centuries before the
Christian formulation was canonically established, a process of
development took place between the two extreme and heretical
opinions of "Tritheism" on the one hand and "Unitarianism"
on the other. In the twelfth century the Calabrian Cister-
cian, Joachim of Flora, fell into the temptation of Tritheism
and was condemned. He claimed that the unity of nature in the
Persons was a collective unity, "as when one says that a multitude of men form a people, and the multitude of faithful, a
Church, as we read in Acts: 'There was one heart and soul in all
the company of believers' (4. 32)".[5] Before him such Mono-
physites as John Philoponus and Stephen Gobarus, Alexan-
drians of the sixth century, claimed that there were three
natures in God, although they claimed to profess only one God.
The followers of Unitarianism were not less numerous. They
wavered between two positions equally opposed to the faith of
the Church: on the one hand, Subordinationism—they placed
the Son and the Spirit below the Father just as the Arians had
done before and the Pneumatomachians (who denied the
divinity of the Holy Spirit); and on the other hand, Modalism—
they made the Father, Son and Holy Spirit diverse aspects of a
unique person who fulfilled different rôles. Sabellius, one of the
authors of this heresy, which is sometimes called after him,
Sabellianism, was condemned by Pope St Callistus. With each
error the Church reacted with renewed vigour and formulated
her beliefs with more precision.

How, then, is the One three, and the Three one?

THREE "PERSONS" IN ONE

To begin with, what are these "three"? There was still no

[5] St Thomas comments on the condemnation of Joachim of Flora in
Opusculum XXXII (Ed. Mandonnet).

common name to indicate them during the first centuries. About the year 215, however, Tertullian applied to them the word "Person": the Son is the "Second Person" and the Spirit, the "Third". The term was later accepted by the Councils of Antioch (362), Rome and Constantinople (382). St Augustine used it, but not too eagerly, it seems, for he writes: "The Father is not the Son, the Son is not the Father; the Holy Spirit is neither the Father nor the Son. They are, therefore, three. . . . But if one were to ask three what, human language shows how poor it is. Someone has answered: three Persons, but not so much to give the answer as not to remain silent."[6] We must admit, he says later, that such terms as person and hypostasis "have been invented of necessity when the objections and errors of heretics have prompted lengthy discussion. The human mind, despite its limitations, strives to express clearly to the understanding of men how in its measure it conceives the Lord its creator (through religious faith or a certain understanding). It is afraid to say three essences, for fear of placing the slightest diversity in the supreme Equality. Yet it is unable to deny that they are three. Sabellius did deny it and fell into heresy. . . . In the search for what the three are, some have said three substances or persons."[7]

The question is not without certain difficulties, for did not the Jews worship God as one Person? St Thomas thought so.[8] Is there in our language nothing more absolute than the term person? Is it not sufficient in and to itself? How will it help to point out the relations in God which properly speaking constitute each divine Person? The Father cannot be defined without the Son; he is a pure act of begetting. Nothing but that distinguishes him from the Son. He is related to the Son to whom he communicates the divine nature, although the Son receives it from him without being in the least inferior to him. In the same way, the Father and the Son are not distinct without

[6] *De Trinitate*, Book V. Chapter 9.
[7] Ibid., Book VIII, Chapter 4.
[8] Cf. *Summa Theol.* IIIª, qu. 3, art. 3, ad 1, ad 2.

the Holy Spirit towards whom they are entirely borne by the Gift which they make of their love. Thus, what we can say of the divine Person is that it is a "subsistent relation", but considered precisely in so far as this relation is "subsistent", as every human person is.

PROCESSION OF LOVE?

But perhaps we have gone too far in speaking of the Father's and the Son's "gift of love", for by it we already suggest that the second procession is a procession of Love. What does this mean?

First of all we say "procession". It is a vague and general term. Whatever passes from one point to another, from one state to another, all movement, every act and order, can be called a "procession". We can state exactly the manner of the first procession, since Scripture tells us that there is a Father and a Son. The Son, then, proceeds from the Father by way of generation. But what is the process, the term of which, if we may so speak, gives rise to the Holy Spirit? Due to our ignorance we do not specify, but rather make use of the general term "procession".

The human mind in its yearning for the understanding and vision of God, will not, however, stop there. We are not completely uninformed on the procession of the Holy Spirit, since in Scripture there is a continuous reference to him, to his activity and his being sent by the Father and by the Son. How, then, distinguish the second procession from the first? St Augustine felt it was beyond him to answer this question: *Nescio, non valeo, non sufficio*—"I do not know, I cannot explain it, it escapes me." St John Damascene felt the same way. In the thirteenth century, at the famous monastic school of Paris, Richard of St Victor taught that the procession of the Holy Spirit is like the "free outpouring between two friends, the Father and the Son, who in their generosity agree to communicate to a third the joy of being loved as they love each other".

Hence, the axiom which exercised such a great influence on the thirteenth century: the first procession is by way of nature, the second from the will.

This axiom seemed ingenious, but it was questionable and in the long run was found unacceptable. St Thomas thinks that both processions are natural, although the will is never absent. He prefers to say that the first procession is carried out by way of the intellect (the speaking or generation of a word is the only action in which the notion of begetting is discernible), while the second is by way of the will. The Holy Spirit is not the fruit of a generation, nor could he be, since there is only one Son— *Unigenitus* (John 1. 14, 18; Heb. 11. 17–19; 1 John 4. 9)—in God.

So the Holy Spirit is the fruit of a procession; what is the nature of this procession?

This question is identical with the preceding one. To describe the nature of this second procession is to explain what he is at the term of the procession. And conversely, to explain what he is, does it not suggest the manner in which he proceeds? It is this point that the reflection of Christians and the formulation of the Magisterium was gradually to develop.

Holy Scripture has left us a great number of names and images for designating and referring to the Holy Spirit; he appears as the Breath of God or as a sigh, as the Finger of God (Exod. 8. 15; Ps. 8. 4; Luke 11. 20 and the parallel passage in Matt. 12. 28), as the Spirit of holiness and sanctification; as the Advocate, he who helps, and the Paraclete. He is addressed under the symbol of fire, living water, unction, chrism, perfume and the dove; he is given by the imposition of hands (Acts 8. 17) or by a breath (John 20. 22). He is a gift, the present of God, the bond of unity. . . . All these symbols try to characterize the Holy Spirit. What do they have in common? Or to put it in another way, what is the source of the actions which all these names call to mind and which would explain them?

The Greek Fathers stopped at the scriptural words and images: the Holy Spirit is the Spirit of holiness, he comes forth from God as a sweet odour . . . they love to say. But is it not possible to discover at our level an intelligible principle which will apply to all these actions of the Holy Spirit such as they have been revealed to us?

St Augustine attempted this; and he is the very first to have discerned Love as the essential characteristic of the Holy Spirit. He observed that Scripture shows us the Holy Spirit as that of the Father and the Son, and also as a gift who pours love into our hearts (Rom. 5. 5):

> Their common spirit, what does this mean? Is it their unity with each other, their holiness, their love? their substantial and eternal communion? their friendship and fellowship . . . ? Yes, we say, it is their mutual charity, the love of the Father for the Son and the Son for the Father. It is by this reciprocal and essential gift that they preserve between them the unity of the Spirit in the bond of peace (Ephes. 4. 3). Thus we know that there can only be three: he who loves his offspring, he who loves his principle, and their love.[9]

He, who is above all "the gift of God" (cf. Rom. 5. 5; Acts 8. 20; 2. 38; 10. 45; 11. 17; Luke 11. 13) is, by an entirely privileged title, love.

We shall return to this basic inquiry. For the moment let us simply dwell on the fact that the Holy Spirit is presented to us as proceeding from the friendship of the Father and the Son. There is a difficulty here. If the Holy Spirit is the mutual friendship of the Father and the Son, he presupposes the Father and the Son, and he necessarily proceeds from each one at the same time: there would be no friendship if there was no friend. The Father, therefore, gives himself to a friend in the person of his Son, and the two of them communicate to a third the joy of their love. Perhaps we could say that this third is the joy of their love: for St Bernard the Holy Spirit is the mutual kiss of the Father and the Son.

Theological thought developed between this position, as is

[9] *De Trinitate*, Book VI, n. 7.

especially evident in the work of the thirteenth-century Richard
of St Victor, and another which, at least apparently, seems to
respect the tradition of the Greeks. This latter was in fact, at
least explicitly since the ninth century, unfavourable to the
Filioque, that is to a procession of the Spirit as proceeding from
the Father and the Son. According to this other point of view,
the Holy Spirit is presented as the love by which the Father
loves himself. God knows himself and in knowing himself he
speaks or begets his Word. In knowing himself God also loves
himself, and in loving himself he "breathes forth the Spirit".

Love, here, proceeds therefore from the Father who, in knowing himself, loves himself. But in loving himself, he loves his
divine essence, and he loves the latter which is one with the
Son, in the Son as well as in himself; likewise the Son loves his
essence in his Father as in himself. Hence we again find St
Augustine's idea, but the perspective is different. Here the
friendship of the Father and the Son is of secondary, not
primary, importance.

THE SPIRIT: ACT OR TERM OF THE SPIRATION?

Let us, however, return to what we have just written: God,
in loving himself, breathes forth the Spirit. What does this
mean? We have already said that the vague term, procession,
is an indication of our embarrassment and the avowed ignorance of theology; it is the same with the verb to breathe. There
is a temptation to present the procession of the Spirit on the
pattern of the procession of the Word. Can this be done? Is
there a "term" in the procession of love as there is a term, the
Word, in the procession of knowledge? Or at least, the term,
the product, what has come forth—since the Holy Spirit comes
forth from the Father—could it not be the act of loving himself? Must we look for a term, a product of this act of loving?
Such are the questions which theology sets itself and within
which it wavers among several possible answers.

In reality, love is not static like the internal word which the thinking man begets. It does not abandon him who loves, to himself and in himself; on the contrary, it draws him and carries him towards the one who is loved. This is one way of looking at it.

But there is another in which love appears in some way, despite all, more static. For love transforms from within him who loves; it changes him by modelling him in some way on him whom he loves.

Thus, on the one hand, love is an impulse, an impulsion, a sighing in the one who loves. Is the Spirit this impulse of the Father for the object of his love? On the other hand, love is the impression of the beloved in the heart of him who loves and where the beloved becomes another self; do we not speak of the feeling of love, the intimacy of love? Love is a mysterious weight of sweetness which makes the heart of the lover heavy with happiness. Should we see the Holy Spirit as this term, this product, this mysterious weight of happiness in the heart of the Father? But, must we sacrifice one of these views to the other? St Thomas did not do so. It is necessary at least to recognize that we may not separate them. If the beloved enters the heart of the lover, if he insinuates himself, if he is "imprinted" upon his heart, it is not without a vital reaction from the lover who willingly succumbs in some way to the attractions, charms or rights of the beloved, and who is henceforth completely turned towards him as towards a new centre of gravitation, activities and joys. And if he who loves has the initiative, his movement will not come to rest until he experiences in himself this admirable preferment of the beloved being impressed upon his heart. Is not the Holy Spirit this living weight of happiness in the heart of God, bent over the Object of his love? This, at least, in so far as a resumé of his work is possible, is what the Portuguese John of St Thomas, one of the most eminent theologians of the seventeenth century, seems to say.

Whatever the verdict on these explanations, we do gain from them the realization that there are many ways of speaking of love in God. God loves himself, and he loves his own goodness;

in the first sense love is an essential attribute of God, it is identical with his essence: "God is Love" (1 John 4. 8, 16).

The Father loves the Son and the Son loves the Father; in this second sense, love is what theology calls a "notional act", that is, an act which "makes known" the active relation by which the Father and the Son are principles of the Spirit, or in other words, what the Father and the Son possess as their own in relation to the Spirit. We say that they breathe forth the Spirit. And finally, in a third sense, Love denotes the Holy Spirit himself; it is therefore a personal name.

PERSON AND RELATION: THE FILIOQUE

The exacting reader will understand that theology cannot stop there and that in fact it has not done so. Other questions arise. The Father is "made known" by his Paternity. If there is also in him an active spiration from which the Spirit proceeds, does this not create a real distinction between the Paternity and the active spiration? St Thomas did not think so by virtue of the principle—without which it is impossible by reason not to see a contradiction between a unity of essence and a trinity of persons—"there is a real distinction between the Persons only by reason of their relative opposition".[10] Hence, where there are two opposed relations, they necessarily result in two persons: paternity and filiation. But where these relations are not opposed, they result in just one person, and they are not really distinct; thus Paternity and active spiration or Filiation and active spiration.

We see the importance of this intuition. A divine Person can be defined only by a relation: Paternity is the Person of the

[10] *Summa Theol.* Ia, qu. 30, art. 2, c. This axiom illustrates or expresses the manner in which the Persons are intimate; each one can be defined only by his relation with the other. This reciprocal intimacy of the Persons between themselves is what Latin theology calls the circumincession of the Persons, and Greek theology, *Perichoresis*. It is rich with consequences in religious psychology; the human person cannot be fully known nor can it open out without its relation to another, nor without its relation to the absolute Other who is God.

Father, Filiation is the Person of the Son, procession (under-stood as the second procession) is the Person of the Holy Spirit. Each Person is the relation which opposes it to the other, in as much as this relation subsists in the unique divine nature.

But we can also see the consequences: since active spiration, by the Father and the Son, is not opposed to the Paternity or Filiation, it is not distinguished from the Father or the Son. If the generation of the Son is proper to the Father, active spiration of the Holy Spirit is common to the Father and the Son.[11]

How did it happen that the East was so opposed to this principle? We cannot refrain from saying a word on this since after twelve centuries the *Filioque* dispute still endures and is sometimes presented as the main discord between the Churches.

Since the time of St Augustine the West insists that "the Holy Spirit proceeds principally from the Father and com-monly from both, i.e. from the Father and the Son",[12] while the East says the Holy Spirit proceeds from the Father through the Son.[13] A diagram of the two formulas would be as follows:

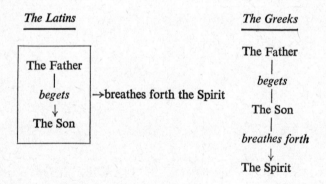

The Latins

The Father
|
begets   →breathes forth the Spirit
↓
The Son

The Greeks

The Father
|
begets
|
The Son
|
breathes forth
↓
The Spirit

[11] St Thomas, *op. cit.* Ia, qu. 30, art. 2, c.
[12] *De Trinitate*, Bk 15, n. 47.
[13] Cf. St John Damascene, *De Fide Orthodoxa*, Bk 1, Chapter 12.

The Greeks first learned of the Latin formula through a synod of Pope Martin I about the year 650. They were surprised by it, but the explanations of St Maximus the Confessor reassured them. The Latins, he said, express in their own language exactly what the Greeks profess: the substantial union of the Father and the Son which means for the Greeks that the Holy Spirit proceeds from the Father through the Son.

St Maximus was not deceiving himself. The future rupture between the Latins and the Greeks was mainly a question of language. "The preposition ἐκ, by which a translation of the Latin *a* is intended, refers to an absolutely first principle; the Latin formula *a patre et filio*, once it is translated into Greek seems therefore to violate the privilege of the Father by placing the Son on the same level. There is no difficulty in Latin (or in English), for the preposition *a* refers to any principle. We can understand the hesitation of the Greeks to go beyond the Damascene formula: the Holy Spirit proceeds not from the Son but through him from the Father: the Father is the sole Author."[14] There is the same hiatus between the Latin *processio* and the Greek which it claims to translate—ἐκπόρευσις. "The Greeks quite logically and on the authority of Scripture reserve this term for an absolutely first beginning; for them it denotes the relation of the Holy Spirit to the Father, the sole Author and source of the whole Trinity."[15]

The fact remains that the *Filioque*, once it was inserted into the Credo, was sung at Mass by the Latins, first in Spain and then, in 796, in all Frankish churches. At Rome, however, the singing of the creed with this addition was authorized only in the eleventh century. The Frankish liturgy was soon known in the East and this provided a fine opportunity, often unfortunately repeated at each renewal of the dispute between East and West, to be scandalized. In 809 Charlemagne's theologians, assembled at Aix-la-Chapelle, tried, but in vain, to have the Greeks condemned and to sanction the addition of the *Filioque*

[14] H. F. Dondaine, *La Trinité*, Vol. II, p. 323.
[15] Ibid.

in the Creed of Nicaea-Constantinople. The pope refused, although he agreed with the doctrine. Later, Gregory X, Eugenius IV, Clement VIII, also refused to require the Greeks to add the *Filioque* to their Creed. This state of affairs has been reached, no doubt, for reasons largely extrinsic to doctrine.

But why does the Latin Church value this doctrine to which it has returned in divers Councils? On what does it rest? It rests, first of all, on a long tradition which dates back to Tertullian, St Hilary and St Ambrose, although St Augustine is the first to have expressly stated it. It also rests on a long and profound meditation which precludes, so it seems, imagining otherwise the relations of the divine Persons and the relations of the two processions, among them. It is true that the Holy Spirit proceeds principally from the Father, since the Father is the origin of the Son, and that the Son has his being from the Father. Hence the Son also has his place in active spiration from the Father. In this regard it is well to complete the Latin formula by the Greek formula. There is between the Father and the Son an order which conditions their common spiration. But we cannot easily deny that there is also an order between the processions: the generation of the Son on the one hand and the procession of the Spirit on the other.

We have said that only a relative opposition could really distinguish the relations or the divine Persons. Breathing the Holy Spirit does not oppose the Father and the Son. It is, therefore, an act which is absolutely common. They work together in this unique act; they form only "one principle, breathing the Spirit by a unique spiration", according to the formula of the Councils of Lyons and Florence. The unique spiration basically presupposes the first procession.

In other words, since the two Persons who proceed are distinguished solely by the fact that the one receives from the other, we can understand the second procession only after the good communicated by the first procession has been received. Only an order of origin between the processions multiplies the processions.

Once again the Augustinian analogy of love seems a fortunate one for explaining the second procession. Only what is known can be loved. The procession of the Spirit presupposes that of the Word, just as love presupposes knowledge.

OTHER QUESTIONS

These are some of the explanations of the data which theology has elaborated through the course of centuries. What has been given here is only an outline showing how problems gradually arose and the first attempts at a solution. A theology of the Holy Spirit ought to develop the points which we have here barely touched: the theology and philosophy of person; the philosophy of relation, substance and subject, and the theology of the divine relations, research on the properties of these Persons, a study of the notional acts and powers, the relationship between the Persons and the divine Essence, and between the Persons themselves; the philosophy of the act of love and the analogical application of this act to the second procession.

THE DESIRE TO UNDERSTAND AND REVERENCE FOR THE WORD OF GOD

From what has already been said, it should be evident that the light of faith does not make all the propositions of the Church equally clear, and that faith demands of us a certain hierarchy of assent, a certain prudence aligned with a resolute reverence for all the Church professes. Cardinal Cajetan said in the sixteenth century that "so long as there is no definition by the Church, when can we say that a given thesis entails a consequence contrary to the faith? It is not enough that many of the learned agree with it, if there are others who disagree. And for that matter we would excuse from heresy and even all sin those who maintain an erroneous opinion, if at their level and according to their lights they decide to follow what to them

seems the most reasonable course, provided all reverence towards the Church is preserved."[16]

This time-honoured effort of believers in their yearning for
the understanding, vision and possession of God is unavoidable
even if it means proceeding cautiously and falteringly and
sometimes unsuccessfully. Faith would be of small worth and
of little merit if it accepted what it hears without seeking to
grasp, assimilate and understand it. A living faith extracts the
Truth from questions and knows neither cessation nor repose
until it has completely found it. This is how the people of God
in its journey towards beatitude, continually comparing its
meditation and experience of the faith with the Word which it
received as a trust in the Church, progresses step by step, by the
assistance of the Holy Spirit, in the consciousness of what it
has received from God. Gradually formulas are elaborated
which help it to reject past errors and guard it from falling into
them again, or which endeavour to bridge the gap between the
mystery of God and the feebleness of human reason or between
the different truths revealed by God, or finally, which make
explicit a word sown in the beginning as a grain in our minds
and which needs only to mature to be well understood.

Yet, no matter how rich the formulations of theology may
be, they will remain subordinate to faith as well as to the light
of faith without which they would be unintelligible, and to the
data of faith without which there would be nothing to hearken
to and understand.

However rich and extensive theological development may
be, there is more in the occurrence of the Incarnation, in the acts
and words of Christ, in his passion and resurrection, in the outpouring of the Spirit at Pentecost: God has come. God has
spoken and acted in this world among us; God has given us his
Spirit that we might understand and live. The libraries of the
world can go on increasing; they will never finish expressing
what has come to pass in all its depths, in all its levels of understanding. But the faith would lose its vitality if it did not

[16] In Ia, qu. 32, art. 4.

continue in its yearning for investigation and understanding—if theology, satisfied with itself, was no longer today and tomorrow in search of new formulations in the language of the men of today and tomorrow.

AN IMPORTANT PERIOD IN THEOLOGICAL THOUGHT: ST THOMAS AQUINAS

During the course of this gradual approximation through the centuries, there does not seem to have been a finer period after the era of the fourth- to the sixth-century Fathers than the twelfth and thirteenth centuries in the West. Surely the finest possible conclusion to this chapter would be to here present some of the fine passages of St Thomas. They are extracts from the seventeenth and nineteenth chapters of the fourth book of the *Contra Gentiles:*

The Holy Spirit is God
Scripture clearly teaches us that the Holy Spirit is God.

To whom if not to God alone do we consecrate our temples? "The Lord is in his holy temple," says the psalm. And Scripture speaks of a temple dedicated to the Holy Spirit: "Surely you know that your bodies are the shrines of the Holy Spirit?" says the Apostle Paul (1 Cor. 6. 19). The Holy Spirit is therefore God. Paul declares a much more remarkable fact in verse 15: "Know you not that your bodies are the members of Christ?"[17] Since Christ is true God it would not be fitting for the members of Christ to be temples of the Holy Spirit if the Holy Spirit was not God.

The sanctification of man is a work which is proper to God. We read in Leviticus (22. 32): "I am the Lord who sanctifies you." Now, it is the Spirit who sanctifies. St Paul says: "You are washed, but you are sanctified, but you are justified in the name of the Lord Jesus Christ and in the Spirit of our God" (1 Cor. 6. 11); and to the Thessalonians (2 Thess. 2. 13): "God has chosen you first-fruits unto salvation in sanctification of the Spirit, and faith of the truth." Hence the Spirit must be God.

[17] Douay version: also in all the following extracts from the *Contra Gentiles.*

As the soul secures natural life for the body, so God brings to this soul the life of justice and holiness. We read in St John (John 6. 57): "As the living Father has sent me, and I live by the Father, so he that eateth me, the same also shall live by me." Now such a life is the work of the Holy Spirit. And in fact we read in the same place: "It is the Spirit that quickeneth" (6. 63); and in the Epistle to the Romans: "If by the Spirit you mortify the deeds of the flesh, you shall live" (8. 13).

To prove his divinity to the Jews who were unable to bear his claim to be equal to God, the Lord declared that he had the power to raise the dead: "As the Father raiseth up the dead, and giveth life," he says, "so the Son also giveth life to whom he will" (John 5. 21). Now the power of restoring life belongs to the Holy Spirit. St Paul says (Rom. 8. 11): "If the Spirit of him, that raised up Jesus from the dead, dwell in you; he that raised up Jesus Christ from the dead, shall quicken also your mortal bodies, because of his Spirit that dwelleth in you." Hence the Holy Spirit is of the divine nature.

We have already shown that creation is the work of God alone. Now, creation belongs properly to the Holy Spirit. "Send forth thy Spirit," says Psalm 103. 30, "and they shall be created." The Book of Job (33. 4) says the same: "The Spirit of God made me." And Ecclesiasticus (1. 9): "He created (wisdom) in the Holy Ghost." The Holy Spirit is thus divine.

St Paul says: "The Spirit searcheth all things, yea, the deep things of God. For what man knoweth the things of a man but the spirit of a man that is in him? So the things also that are of God no man knoweth but the Spirit of God" (1 Cor. 2. 10–11). No creature understands the depths of God; does not the Lord himself say so? "No one knoweth the Son, but the Father; neither doth anyone know the Father, but the Son" (Matt. 11. 27); and we read in Isaias (24. 16) that God says: "My secret to myself." Hence the Holy Spirit is not a creature.

Furthermore, according to the aforesaid comparison of St Paul, the Holy Spirit acts in regard to God as the spirit of man is to man. Now man's spirit is within him and intrinsic; it is not of a different nature but something that belongs to him. Thus the Spirit of God is not of a nature that is foreign to God.

Moreover, if someone wants to compare the aforesaid text of

Isaias (64. 4) he will clearly see that the Spirit is God. For Isaias says: "Eye hath not seen, O God, besides thee, what things thou hast prepared for them that wait for thee." St Paul in quoting this adds: "The Spirit searcheth the deep things of God" (1 Cor. 2. 9). It is thus manifest that the Spirit knows the depths of God, "which the Spirit has prepared for those who hope in him." And if no one has seen these things except God as Isaias says, it is clear that the Holy Spirit is God.

Isaias says further: "I heard the voice of the Lord saying: Whom shall I send? and who shall go for us? And I said: . . . Send me! And he said: Go, and thou shalt say to this people: Hearing hear and understand not!" (6. 8–9). St Paul ascribes these words to the Holy Spirit when speaking to the Jews, for he cries out to them: "Well did the Holy Ghost speak to our fathers by Isaias the prophet saying: Go to this people and say to them: With the ear you shall hear, and shall not understand" (Acts 28. 25–26). It is thus clear that the Holy Spirit is God.

According to Scripture it is God who spoke by the prophets. The author of the Book of Numbers, speaking for God, says: "If there be among you a prophet, I will appear to him in a vision or I will speak to him in a dream" (12. 6), and in one of the psalms we sing: "I will hear what the Lord God will speak to me" (84. 9). This clearly shows that the Holy Spirit has spoken through the prophets. And still another witness, the Acts: "The Scripture must needs be fulfilled, which the Holy Ghost spoke before by the mouth of David" (1. 16). And the Lord himself in St Mark: "How do the Scribes say, that Christ is the Son of David? For David saith by the Holy Ghost: The Lord said to my Lord: sit on my right hand" (Mark 12. 35–6; cf. Matt. 22. 43–4). And finally, Peter writes: "For prophecy came not by the will of man at any time; but the holy men of God spoke, inspired by the Holy Ghost" (2 Peter 1. 21). All the Scriptures agree in attesting that the Holy Spirit is God.

The revelation of mysteries belongs properly to God as Scripture tells us: "There is a God in heaven that revealeth mysteries" (Dan. 2. 28). Yet St Paul presents the revelation of mysteries as a work proper to the Holy Spirit: "To us that God hath revealed them by his Spirit" (1 Cor. 2. 10). So we see again that the Holy Spirit is God.

It belongs to God to teach man from within. Yet, Scripture says that it is he who teaches man understanding (Ps. 93. 10), who gives "wisdom to the wise and knowledge to them that have understanding" (Daniel 2. 21). St John too shows that this is the peculiar work of the Holy Spirit: "The Paraclete, the Holy Ghost, whom the Father will send in my name, he will teach you all things" (John 14. 26). So the Holy Spirit is divine.

Where there is identity of action there is identity of nature. There is one action of the Son which is the same as that of the Holy Spirit: to speak to the hearts of the saints: "Do you seek a proof of Christ that speaketh in me?" (2 Cor. 13. 3). But it is clear that the Holy Spirit does the same: "It is not you who shall speak, but the Spirit of your Father who will speak in you." There is thus identity of nature between the Son and the Holy Spirit, and consequently between them and the Father, since we have shown that the Father and the Son have a unique nature.

It is God's privilege to dwell in the souls of the saints: "You are", says St Paul, "the temple of the living God; as God saith: I will dwell in them" (2 Cor. 6. 16). The same is said of the Holy Spirit: "Know you not that you are the temple of God, and that the Spirit of God dwelleth in you?" (1 Cor. 3. 16). Therefore the Holy Spirit is God.

It is likewise God's privilege to be everywhere. "Do I not", says God by the mouth of Jeremias, "fill heaven and earth?" (23. 24). This is also the privilege of the Holy Spirit: "The Spirit of the Lord hath filled the whole world," says the Book of Wisdom (1. 7); and in the Psalm there is written: "Whither shall I go from thy Spirit, whither shall I flee from thy face? If I ascend into heaven, thou art there" (138. 7–8). And the Lord said to his disciples: "You shall receive the power of the Holy Ghost . . . and you shall be witnesses . . . in Jerusalem, and in all Judea, and Samaria, and even to the uttermost part of the earth" (Acts 1. 8). We must conclude then that the Holy Spirit is everywhere. It is he who dwells in the hearts of men who are scattered over the whole surface of the earth. Hence the Holy Spirit is God.

The Holy Spirit is explicitly called God in Scripture. Peter said to Ananias: "Why hath Satan tempted thy heart, that thou shouldst lie to the Holy Ghost?" (Acts 5. 3)? And he adds: "Thou hast not lied to men but to God" (5. 4). Thus the Holy Spirit is God.

To grant divine adoption is the act of God alone. No spiritual creature is called a son of God by reason of its nature but by the grace of adoption. That is why St Paul ascribes this work to the Son of God who is true God: "God has sent his Son that we might receive the adoption of sons" (Gal. 4. 5). The Holy Spirit is the cause of our adoption: "You have received the Spirit of adoption of sons, whereby we cry: Abba, Father" (Rom. 8. 15). The Spirit is thus not a creature but God.

If the Holy Spirit is not God, then he must be a creature. Now, it is obvious that he is not a corporeal creature. Neither is he a spiritual creature; no spiritual creature is infused into the inmost parts of another creature since a creature is not participated in but is rather a participant. The Holy Spirit is infused into the inmost souls of the saints and they participate in him, so to speak. We read that Christ was full of the Spirit (Luke 4. 1), and the Apostles as well (Acts 2. 4).

If anyone should claim that the aforesaid works which belong to God are ascribed to the Holy Spirit, not under the supreme title, as God, but under the title of magisterial service, as of a creature, then the error of such an opinion would be manifestly clear from the words of St Paul: "There are diversities of operations but the same God, who worketh all in all" (1 Cor. 12. 6). Then he adds after having enumerated the various gifts of God: "One and the same Spirit worketh (all these things) dividing to every one as he will" (12. 11). He clearly indicates here that the Holy Spirit is God since he attributes to him works which are absolutely proper to God and he grants that they are accomplished according to his good pleasure. It is, therefore, evident that the Holy Spirit is God.

How to understand what is said about the Holy Spirit

Instructed by the inspired words of the sacred Scriptures, we firmly maintain that the Holy Spirit is truly God, subsistent and personally distinct from the Father and Son. We must now consider, to the extent that we are able, how this truth is to be understood, that we might thereby defend it against the attacks of unbelievers.

We must at the start recall that in every intellectual nature there must be a will. The understanding passes to the act of knowing, thanks to an intelligible form which informs it, just as in nature a thing is in act because of its proper form. Now the natural thing, through its proper form which perfects it in its species, has that which moves it to the operations proper to it and towards its proper end which it attains through these acts. Hence, the adage: As a being is, so it will act. It tends towards that which is suitable to it according to its nature. Hence, from the intelligible form there results in the intelligent being an inclination to its proper operations and end. Now, in an intellectual nature this inclination is called the will; and it is the will which is the principle of the operations in us by which the being endowed with an intellectual nature acts in view of its end; the end and good being the very object of the will. Thus where there is an intellectual nature, there is a will.

But the will has many acts, e.g. desire, delight, hate, etc. Of all these acts, the principal one, the one underlying them all, is love. The following explanation will help in understanding this: The will is related to a being with an intellectual nature as a natural inclination is related to a natural being, an inclination which we call the natural appetite. This inclination of nature is present in each thing in such a way that this thing possesses a form, the principle of its inclination, which determines the affinity and harmony with the term towards which the thing is moved. Thus, for example, a heavy body has a certain affinity and harmony with "the below" towards which it falls. In the same way every inclination of the will arises from the fact that through the intelligible form something is apprehended and appraised as fitting and attractive for the subject. But to be attracted towards something is to love it. Hence, every inclination of the will and even of the sensible appetite has its origin in love. As soon as we love anything, regardless of what it is, we desire it if the object of our love is absent; we rejoice when it is present; we are sad when we are kept from attaining it; we hate and are angry with everything that separates us from it.

Hence we see that what is loved is not only found in the thought of him who loves, but also, although in another manner, in his will. In thought the object loved is found in its natural resemblance; but in the will of the one loving, the object loved exists as the term of the movement already exists in the being in movement towards a term to which it is proportioned and adapted. Thus, for example, "height" is, in a way, present in fire since by virtue of its lightness, fire is completely proportioned and adapted for this place. On the contrary, the fire which is kindled is present in the fire which kindles it, according to the likeness of its form.

Since there is a will in every intellectual nature, there must be a will in God for he is an intellectual nature. Yet it does not follow that the will in God is a reality that is added to his Essence (or nature), nor that his intellect is as we have shown. God's will is God's very substance. And since the divine intellect is also the very substance of God, it follows that in God the intellect and the will are one and the same thing. We have explained elsewhere how it is clear that what is complex in creatures is simple in God.

And since we have shown that the action of God is God's very essence, and his essence is his will, it follows that in God there is no possible, virtual or habitual will, but only an actual will. Thus, since we have shown that every act of the will has its roots in love, love is necessarily in God.

We now advance a step further: We have already seen that the proper object of the divine will is his goodness. It is thus absolutely clear that God loves primarily and principally his goodness, i.e. himself. And since the object loved exists in a certain way in the will of the one loving, if God is loved by himself, he must be present in his will in the same way as the loved one is present to the lover. Now the loved one is in the lover according as he is loved; and to love is a certain desire. And since God's desire, like his will, is the very existence of God, it follows that if God exists in his will by way of love, this existence is not, as in us, accidental but an essential existence. In other words, God as present in the loving will of God is truly and substantially God.

When we consider a being which is in the will in the same way that the beloved is in him who loves, we discover in it a double relation: firstly, to what is conceived by the intellect and secondly, to the reality itself, of which the intellectual conception is the expression or word. Nothing is loved unless it is first known. But it is not simply the knowledge of the beloved that is loved, but the beloved in as much as he is good. It follows that the love, in virtue of which God exists in his will as the beloved in the lover, proceeds both from the Word of God and from God whom the word expresses.

We have, moreover, seen that the presence of the beloved in the lover is not verified in its specific likeness as the presence of the known in the knower. Yet, what proceeds by way of generation, proceeds precisely as a natural likeness of that from which it proceeds. We ought thus to say that the process which makes the thing exist in the will, as the beloved in the lover, does not have the nature of a generation as the process which makes the thing exist in the intellect. Consequently, if God proceeds by way of love, he does not proceed as engendered, and thus cannot be called Son.

The beloved exists in the will as an inclination which draws the will as a force which in some way intrinsically impels the lover towards the beloved. Now, in all living beings the impulse which comes from within liberates the breath or vital spirit. This is why it is fitting that God, who proceeds by way of love, bear the name Spirit, since he proceeds by way of a breath or spiration. This is why St Paul attributes to the Spirit and to Love a certain power of impulsion: Those who are sons of God, are led by the Spirit, he says to the Romans (8. 14). And to the Corinthians: "The charity of Christ presseth us" (2 Cor. 5. 14).

If all movement is denoted by its term, then, since the love in question is he by whom God himself is loved, it is fitting to give the name Holy Spirit to God proceeding by way of love. All that is consecrated to God or attributed to him is called holy.

CHAPTER VI

THE NAMES AND ATTRIBUTES OF THE HOLY SPIRIT

He whom we call the Holy Spirit has already appeared under a number of names. He is first of all the *Breath* of God, and so he remains through the whole biblical tradition, even though in the end the meaning of the word must be purified of every connotation incompatible with God. He is also the *Life*, the *Gift*, the *Paraclete*, the *Seal* of unity, the *Sanctifier*, the *Vivifier*.

Moreover, we find in the New Testament many trinitarian formulas (Ephes. 4. 3–6; 2 Cor. 13. 13) which seem to ascribe a particular rôle as proper to each Person not only in relation to another Person, but also in relation to the governing of the world and spirits. In 1 Corinthians (12. 4–6) St Paul seems to attribute charisms and spiritual gifts to the Spirit, services to the Lord, "manifestations of power" or miracles (1 Cor. 6. 14) to God. In many places the name God is given to the Father (cf. Acts 10. 38; Rom. 1. 1–7; Heb. 9. 14), Lord to Christ, and Spirit to the third Person. The work of sanctification is generally attributed to the Holy Spirit (Rom. 15. 16; 1 Cor. 6. 11; 1 Peter 1. 2; 3. 18; Apoc. 1. 6; 22. 1), as well as knowledge of God's secrets (1 Cor. 2. 11). The Holy Spirit is also said to dwell in us: our bodies are temples of the Holy Spirit (1 Cor. 6. 19). He constitutes the "foretaste" (2 Cor. 1. 22) of our heritage, communicates the adoption of sons (Gal. 4. 6), draws us into the unity of the Son and gives us access to the Father (Ephes. 2. 18; 4. 3); he regenerates and renews us (Titus 3. 5), bestows upon us the power to confess Christ (1 John 4. 2); he is a "river of life" (Apoc. 22. 1; cf. John 14. 19). It is also he who establishes the pastors of the Church of God (Acts 20. 28), who is "for ever with the disciples" (John 14. 16). It is in the Spirit that Christ offers himself to God (Heb. 9. 14).

In rereading these Epistles and the texts that we have quoted, it will be seen how accurate was that intuition of Augustine's which the whole of tradition adopted: the Holy Spirit is Love. Love is the outstanding characteristic of all the activities which seem to be peculiar to him.

And yet, to say that there is no Love in the works of the Father or in the works of the Son would be untrue and blasphemous, and opposed to Scripture as well. St Paul ends his second letter to the Corinthians with the words: "The grace of our Lord Jesus Christ, and the love of God, and the imparting of the Holy Spirit be with you all." Clearly, grace is here attributed to the Lord Jesus and Love to the Father. Elsewhere, to the Philippians, he again writes: "If anything is meant by encouragement in Christ, by loving sympathy, by common fellowship in the Spirit" (2. 1), where Love seems also to designate the Father. However, these expressions are rare. Yet, their existence is sufficient to warrant a question: What do these names, these attributes, these rôles which are given to the Holy Spirit, signify? What do they represent? What can we say about them?

EACH PERSON IS A RELATION

To begin with let us recall that only the relations of origin distinguish the three Persons in God. All activities *ad extra*, those which God produces outside himself, are therefore common to the Trinity. Thus, for example, to attribute creation to the Father in such a way that it is the work of the Father alone and not that of the Son or the Spirit, necessarily diminishes the

Son and the Spirit. This is the error into which Arius fell; he placed the Son below the Father and made a creature of him. God creates by his essence or nature, and his essence is common to the Father, the Son and the Spirit. There is nothing wanting to the divine nature of the Son nor that of the Holy Spirit. Since the three Persons have only one nature and only one being, they consequently have only one power and one operation. Whether it be in the natural order, in the order of divine adoption, or even in that of the Incarnation, the production of any created effect whatever, is common to the whole Trinity.[1] This affirmation has often been reiterated by Councils to avert the errors of the Arians and those of their successors. "We believe", declared the Council of Toledo in 675, "that the Father, the Son and the Holy Spirit have the same substance; yet we do not say that the Virgin Mary begot the unity of the Trinity, but only the Son who alone assumed our nature into the unity of his Person. And we believe that even the Incarnation of the Son of God is the work of the whole Trinity because the operations of the Trinity are inseparable."[2] St Thomas states even more clearly: "The three Persons caused the human nature to be united to the one Person of the Son."[3] All the acts of Christ, although they are in fact acts which have Christ as their subject, in their causality, inasmuch as they are created, depend on the three Persons who give Christ the power to perform these acts and cause them in him (on their own level and in their own way as first cause) but in such a way that they are his.

What is absolutely proper to the Father is thus to be Father, and not to have the initiative, the authority, the power of creating that certain texts—which we must seek to understand —seem, however, to attribute to him. What is proper to the

---

[1] Cf. Council of Toledo, 675 (Denz. 284): "The operations of the Trinity are inseparable". Cf. also St Thomas Aquinas, *Summa Theol.* IIIa, qu. 23, art. 2.

[2] Denzinger, *op. cit.*, n. 284. Cf. also 254, 428, etc.

[3] *Summa Theol.* IIIa, qu. 3, art. 4 c .

Son is to be the Son. And what is proper to the Spirit is to be breathed by the Father and the Son.

APPROPRIATED ATTRIBUTES

How then, in these circumstances, are we to understand the words of Jesus on the "Paraclete", or the Epistles of St Paul which in general grant the Holy Spirit the privilege of justifying and sanctifying our souls?

Latin theology has taken a big step towards the understanding of these revealed truths by distinguishing three kinds of attributes in God: the *essential* attributes, those which pertain to the divine nature as such and thus are common to the three Persons: Lord, Ruler, Omnipotent, Creator, Wise, Understanding, Loving; the *personal* attributes which pertain to one Person alone, namely the relative attributes: Father, Son or Word, or Image of God, Gift or Breath breathed by the Father and the Son; and finally the *appropriated* attributes which are the essential and common attributes, but used to indicate one of the Persons in his own right. Thus, as we have seen, the Father is sometimes called Creator or even God in St Paul, the Son, Wisdom or Truth, and the Holy Spirit is designated by Mercy or Power of holiness. Are we not in the habit, for example, of calling Rome "the City" although this name is obviously not proper to it? This is a kind of "appropriation".

Once started on this path, through their knowledge of Scripture and Christian tradition, the Fathers and Doctors of the Church and certain authors of liturgical texts, have multiplied or rather transcribed under various forms the appropriations of the New Testament. We may be confident that a very sure spiritual instinct guided them and that, especially where the liturgy has retained these formulas, they were according to "the mind of the Church".

Thus St Hilary can write: *Aeternitas in Patre, Species in Imagine, Usus in Munere,*[4] Eternity is in the Father, Beauty in

[4] *De Trinitate 2.*

the Image (the Son), and fruition in the Gift (the Holy Spirit). St Augustine[5] understands the three causalities referred to in 1 Cor. 8. 6 as appropriations: *Ex quo* (*omnia*) (the Father), *Per quem* (the Son) and *In quo* (the Holy Spirit): from whom, through whom and in whom. St Bernard names the Trinity: Unity, Truth and Goodness. All kinds of appropriations are possible whether they arise from created effects which necessarily refer to the three Persons indivisibly, the divine attributes common to the three Persons, or the divine gifts, natural or supernatural. So, from the last point of view, an appropriation is what ascribes creation to the Father, re-creation to the Son and glorification to the Spirit, or creation to the Father, the ordering of things to the Wisdom of the Son and salvation to the Mercy and Goodness of the Spirit. "Although every created effect proceeds from every attribute of God", says St Thomas, "nevertheless, each effect can be reduced to that effect with which it has, according to its nature, a certain affinity. Thus we attribute the order in things to Wisdom, the justification of a Sinner to the Mercy and Goodness pouring itself out 'superabundantly' (Rom. 5. 20; 1 Tim. 1. 14; etc.); as to creation which is in production of the very substance of things, it can be reduced to Power."[6]

Appropriation is thus based on an affinity or privileged similarity between some *essential attribute*, for example, Wisdom, and some *personal* property (the Word of the Father). It is by virtue of such an affinity that we appropriate Wisdom to the Word. In the same way we appropriate Power to the Father because power has a certain affinity with the Principle, and Goodness, Mercy and Joy, to the Holy Spirit, because these attributes have a certain affinity with the Love which proceeds from the Father and the Son.

Are we, however, going to maintain that the Father is Wise only "through" the Wisdom which he begets "as though the Son alone was Wisdom, and that the title "wise" is not applicable

---

[5] *De Trinitate* 6, Chap. 10.
[6] *Summa Theol.* Ia, qu. 45, art. 6, ad 3.

to the Father considered independently of the Son, but only to the Father and the Son taken together? The Son is indeed called the Wisdom of the Father because he is the Wisdom born of the Father who is himself Wise. Each of them is in himself wisdom, and the two together form only one wisdom. Hence, the Father is not Wise through the Wisdom which he begets, but by the Wisdom which is his essence."[7] It is in this sense that we sing in the Credo at Mass: *Lumen de lumine*: the Son is the Light, born of Light. And what we say of the Father and Son is equally true when speaking of the Holy Spirit. The Father and the Son do not love "by a personal Love" which is the Holy Spirit in such a way that without the Holy Spirit they would not love and would not have love in them. The Father is Love, the Son is Love, the Holy Spirit is Love born of Love. But precisely because he is born of the Father and the Son in the manner in which the impulse of love proceeds from the spirit of one who loves, love, goodness, mercy, "consolation" are especially appropriated to the Holy Spirit. And thus the use of appropriation is justified: to make us know and in some way to make familiar and more "personal"—with respect to us—the divine Persons; to acquaint us with them in such a way that when we see them face to face we may recognize them without ever having seen them, because of a long acclimatization, so to speak, and the tutelage of faith.

It is a great pity when the theologian, somehow overawed by his own findings, misunderstands or neglects appropriation, seeing in it nothing more than "scholarly play", "a fortunate accommodation" which explains nothing. He knows very well, but then he knows too well, that every divine perfection is common to the three Persons. This is the "too easy triumph of reason, where theology gives way to its own successes; the desire for clarity in the service of the unity of Essence runs the risk of undervaluing the means which faith uses to lay siege to the mystery".[8]

[7] St Thomas, *op. cit.* Ia, qu. 39, art. 7, ad 2.
[8] H. F. Dondaine, *op. cit.* Vol. 2, p. 420.

We must not think that we have understood everything because we have understood something—the unity in operation of the three Persons. God speaks more secretly, more mysteriously and his language is not less divine because we do not immediately find there the clarity, the pallid, limited clarity, of our reason. It is significant that God has constantly used appropriations. It is because he has something to say to us: "The language of the Scriptures, the Councils, the Fathers, the unanimity of the theologians using appropriation to clarify the relations within the Trinity and to describe the relations of the divine Persons with us, form in this connection the most imposing, most authoritative and even the most detailed of testimonies."[9]

Let us, therefore, seriously consider these "attributes" of the Persons which the sacred writers have left us, and after them, with them, the whole Tradition of the Church. Even if we still do not know, in spite of the longing of our faith which never ceases trying to comprehend it, the manner in which appropriation fits each Person, we still know that it *is* fitting. This is enough to make us respect it and carefully guard it and not to speak carelessly of the divine Persons, ascribing, for example, mercy to the Father, love to the Son, Wisdom and Understanding to the Holy Spirit, under the pretext that since these attributes are essential, and the Essence unique, each Person possesses all the qualities. This is true, though it is equally true that our adoptive filiation refers to the Father, the Son and the Holy Spirit, since it corresponds in us to a created effect. But Scripture never says, however, that the Spirit is our Father. What benefit would there be in our having said it, or at least—for it can be profitable to say it once—in our being accustomed to say it? It would be contrary to the divine tutelage which has never spoken thus to us. We should lose our way on the paths that we should make for ourselves, but not on those which God has prepared to lead us to the encounter with himself, the Father, Son and Spirit, yet one nevertheless. In the

[9] A. Gardeil, *La Vie Spirituelle*, July–August 1932, p. 13.

liturgy we are wont to say Our Father when we address the Father of our Lord Jesus Christ, and to call upon him through the Son in the unity of the Holy Spirit. We should follow it in its certainty as well as in its circumspection. May these "appropriations" of the Persons, both in the titles which we give to them and in the "vestiges", "images" and "missions" which we attribute to them, be so familiar to us that the Persons become so too.

Now that the appropriations have been explained, we try to present the various titles, names or attributes which the Church gives to the Holy Spirit by appropriation so as to familiarize ourselves with his mysterious Person.

The Church, in her liturgy, applies various names to the Holy Spirit which are familiar to Christians. We begin by recalling some of these significant names.

Now the Holy Spirit possesses two eminent titles in our adoration and devotion: we worship him as he who forms, and is, the Unity of the Church, and also as he who is the adornment of the sanctified soul to which he distributes his seven gifts. We shall then look at the privileged titles which belong to the Holy Spirit in his rôle as soul of the Church and author of the "seven gifts".

THE TITLES OF THE HOLY SPIRIT IN LITURGY AND TRADITION

The pious memory of the Church has collected the attributes appropriated to the Holy Spirit in numerous hymns, both in the Latin and Oriental liturgies. They vie in beauty. We recall only the two best known: the sequence: *Veni Sancte Spiritus*, from the Mass of Pentecost, and the *Veni Creator* which the Roman Rite uses for Vespers and Terce on the same day.

"*Veni Sancte Spiritus*"
  Come, Holy Spirit, and send a ray of light from on high.
  Come, Father of the poor, Come, Giver of all gifts, Come, Light of men's hearts.

The best Comforter, delightful Guest of the Soul, sweet refreshment,

Rest in toil, appeasement in the mid-day heat, Solace for tears.

O blessed Light, fill in their inmost parts, the hearts of the faithful!

Without your Favour, there is nothing in man, and nothing is guiltless.

Wash what is soiled, water what is dry, heal what is wounded,

Soften what is stiff, warm what is cold, direct what has strayed;

Grant your faithful who confide in you the sevenfold and sacred gift;

Grant the merit of virtue, grant a blessed end, grant eternal joy!

"Veni Creator"

Come, Spirit, Creator, Visit the souls of those who are yours; fill with grace from on high the hearts you have created.

You who are named Paraclete, Gift of God most high, living Spring, Fire, Love, spiritual Unction.

You are the sevenfold Gift, the Finger of God's right hand; you are the solemn promise of the Father; you enrich our mouths with the gift of the Word.

Enkindle a light in our minds, pour love into our hearts, and fortify with constant vigour the weaknesses of our bodies.

Push the enemy far from us, and give us continuous peace; so that being guarded by you we may avoid all that is harmful.

Grant that through you we may know the Father as well as the Son, and that we may believe at all times, in you, the Spirit of them both.

Glory to the Father and to the Son and to the Holy Spirit, and may the Son send us the Gifts of the Spirit.

Let us remember the sweetness, gentleness and joy of these hymns—expressed with still more clarity in others—which the Holy Spirit always diffuses and which are, as it were, linked with his name.

Tradition

But the liturgy is not alone in mysteriously outlining the personality of the Spirit for us. The writings of the saints, even if they do not all have the same value, must also be considered, each one to the degree of authority conferred on it by the status of its author.

Thus, for example, St Thomas discerns in the Holy Spirit the rôle of expressing or manifesting invisible realities. When he wants to show that it is fitting to attribute the conception of the Word Incarnate to the Holy Spirit, he writes:

> The word which we conceive in our intellect is invisible, but it becomes sensible when it is uttered exteriorly by the voice. So, also, the Word of God, conceived in an eternal conception, exists invisibly in the heart of the Father, but by the Incarnation he is made visible to us. The Incarnation of the Word of God is analogous to the vocal expression of our internal word. For the vocal expression of our word is realized by our breath which forms the sound of our word. It was fitting, therefore, to attribute to the Breath, to the Spirit of the Son of God, the formation of his flesh.[10]

In general St Thomas ascribes the goodness in the work of creation and the life of grace in the re-creation to the Holy Spirit:

> Power is attributed and appropriated to the Father, and since power is above all manifest in the creation, we attribute the title Creator to the Father; Wisdom is appropriated to the Son since every artisan works with his intelligence. Do we not say of the Son: By him all things were made (John 1. 3)? As to the Holy Spirit, we ascribe goodness to him, which refers to the divine government which leads all things to their proper end, and the gift of life, since life consists in a certain movement which comes from within; goodness—and the end—is the first principle of movement.[11]

In the re-creation, adoption, "although common to the whole Trinity, is, however, appropriated to the Father as its author, to the Son as its Exemplar and to the Holy Spirit as he who imprints the likeness of this exemplar in us."[12]

[10] *Contra Gentiles*, Bk 4, 46.
[11] *Summa Theol*. Ia, qu. 45, art. 6, ad 2.
[12] *Ibid*. IIIa, qu. 23, art. 2, ad 3.

However, our examination of the Church's tradition would not be complete if we did not also take into account the rites and gestures through which the Spirit is transmitted or which accompany his communication. These rites are, in fact, signs which indicate and express what is communicated.

Especially bear in mind the *breathing* at baptism, *imposition of hands* in confirmation and Orders, the *anointing* at baptism, confirmation and Orders, the *kiss* of peace which accompanies, in particular, the conferring of the sacrament of confirmation. In connection with the imposition of hands, it should be recalled, in order to understand it better, that originally this gesture often signified the transmission of life. It is thus that Jesus placed his hands on the sick (Mark 6. 5; Luke 13. 13) and that his disciples do the same (Mark 16. 18).

All these images, figures, attributions, turn, as we see, on two titles which St Thomas likewise acknowledges as "personal" names of the Holy Spirit: Love and Gift. He writes:

> A gift, properly speaking, is a giving without anything in return, i.e. a giving without the hope of reward. A true gift implies gratuity. Now, for what reason do we give gratuitously unless it be that we love? If, in fact, we do give something gratuitously to another, it is because we desire his well-being, which is another way of saying we love him. So the first thing we give him is love in as much as we desire his well-being. Thus love is the first gift in virtue of which all gratuitous gifts are given. And since it is established that the Holy Spirit proceeds as Love, he proceeds also as a first gift. St Augustine says: The particular gifts which are distributed to the members of Christ come from the gift which is the Holy Spirit.[13]

THE SPIRIT WHO GIVES LIFE AND UNIFIES

There is an extremely intimate relation between the Holy Spirit and the Church which no explanation can bring out completely, no image perfectly illustrate and which no formula can adequately express. We can say that the Church is constituted

[13] *Ibid.* Ia, qu. 38, art. 2.

efficaciously by the Spirit. "Where the Church is," says St Irenaeus, "there also is the Spirit of God; and where the Spirit of God is, there also is the Church and the plenitude of Grace." According to the Apostles' Creed, creation is attributed to the Father, the work of redemption to the Son, and the Church to the Holy Spirit: "I believe in the Holy Spirit, the Holy Catholic Church. . . ."

The Messias came, filled with the Holy Spirit. He laid the foundations of the Church, defined its organization and instituted the sacraments. Then he sent the Spirit who, like the breath of Yahweh causing a commotion among the dry bones in Ezechiel's prophecy, gave life to the institution which Jesus founded. Christ set the structure in place, sent the apostles and instituted the sacramental signs for imparting the grace of the Spirit. Then came the Spirit, animating and organizing the institution from within. The Spirit is within the Church; he is her life and unity. And it is in order to communicate to her this life that Christ came and departed: "It is better for you I should go away, he who is to befriend you will not come to you unless I do go" (John 16. 7). We note that when, in their office as leaders of the Church, the apostles speak, it is difficult to distinguish what comes from the Church and what from the Spirit. At the conclusion of the first council at Jerusalem they wrote: "It is the Holy Spirit's pleasure and ours . . ." (Acts 15. 28). When St Luke gives the account of the missionary commission of Saul and Barnabas, he not only writes that the brethren at Antioch "laid their hands on them, and so took leave of them" (Acts 13. 3) but that "sent on their travels by the Holy Spirit, they went . . ." (Acts 13. 4). As a life-giving wind which brings in its path dew, blessings, fruitfulness and makes the earth germinate, thus the wind of God, which is the Holy Spirit, brings spiritual fruitfulness to the humanity with which it comes in contact, namely the Church.

The Church of the Spirit—the Church to which the Spirit gives life and unity—does not cease to be as well the Church of Christ. The work which the Holy Spirit executes "is not his own work, an independent and completely autonomous work; it is the work *of Christ*—who has already fulfilled the work of the Father, taught the Father's doctrine, etc. The Spirit consecrates and sanctifies the apostles *of Christ*; he not only recalls *Christ's* teaching, but makes it intelligible. 'He will not utter a message of his own. ... He will ... recall to your minds everything I have said to you' (John 16. 13; 14. 26); he brings about sanctification through the sacraments of Christ."[14] It is Christ who sends the Holy Spirit, and the latter is, between the resurrection of Christ and his final parousia, *Dei villicus, Christi vicarius* (Tertullian), God's steward and the representative of Christ. Thus, through the Spirit, the glorious and absent Christ is in the midst of his own, even to the end of time (Matt. 28. 20). The Holy Spirit progressively makes Christ's teaching present in the very depth of the heart and in the deepest level of the understanding.

The Spirit is Christ's dowry to his Church, the "foretaste" (2 Cor. 1. 22) of the heavenly heritage, the mystical ring through which the Church is engaged to her divine Spouse. Note especially that the Spirit is not only the sign of the Covenant, but the very Covenant through which the Church is united to Christ and lives in him, and Christ is united to the Church and lives in her. Without the Spirit the life of Christ "would be that of a mere historical character and the memory of his glorification would be at most an historical fact".[15] Through the Spirit, it is otherwise; Jesus lives among his own. "He is really present here below just as he was in his mortal life, although in another manner: he is no longer present in his body, but through his Spirit. By the gift of the Spirit the mystery of the Word Incarnate remains actual and always efficacious. By the gift of the Spirit, the Master perpetuates in the heart of the Church a lordly spiritual presence, demanding, exacting,

[14] Yves M.-J. Congar, *Si vous êtes mes témoins* (Paris, Ed. du Cerf. 1959), p. 31.
[15] L. M. Dewailly, "L'Esprit et les chrétiens dans l'Église du Christ", p. 72 in *Le Saint-Esprit, auteur de la Vie Spirituelle* (Paris, Ed du Cerf, 1944).

inextinguishable, which makes all the faithful the very members of his body."[16]

It is as impossible to belong to Christ without belonging to the Church, or to belong to the Church without belonging to Christ, as it is impossible to be animated by the Spirit without being in the Church or be truly in the Church without being sanctified by the Spirit. The graces and charisms which the Spirit communicates to each one are the principles of its inwardness and organic relationship with the whole body of which each one, in his own right and place, is a member. In the Spirit there is no opposition but rather an intimate and profound liaison between one's personal life and the life of union with the whole body. Each person here is at the same time the member of a body—the Body of Christ—and has a personal and special function only because he is gathered into the life of the whole Body and participates in it. St Paul says, "the revelation of the Spirit is imparted to each, to make the best advantage of it" (1 Cor. 12. 7). If you are a bishop and pastor of the flock, it is "the Holy Spirit has made you bishops" (Acts 20. 28). If you have the gift of tongues or the gift to interpret them (1 Cor. 12. 10), it is the Holy Spirit you have received for the benefit of all. If you have the gift of contemplation, the whole Church profits from it in the same Spirit who animates the whole Body and places each member in union with all the others.

There is no opposition between the Spirit and the authority in the Church. Authority itself is a gift of the Spirit, and every gift of the Spirit, if it is truly from the Spirit, disposes one to acknowledge and be submissive to it. The enthusiasm of the truly spiritual man is exactly the opposite of "insubordinate illuminism". One and the same Spirit fills all, "awakens spontaneities and controls their harmony".[17] More than all others, the apostles, the heads of the Church, "received power from the Holy Spirit to be witnesses of the risen Christ. More than all

[16] L. M. Dewailly, *op. cit.*, p. 73.
[17] L. M. Dewailly, *op. cit.*, p. 70.

others, they are the inspired ones, and this by reason of their hierarchical rôle."[18]

This does not mean that every vocation and mission as well comes immediately from the hierarchy and is made manifest by it. On the contrary, very often the vocation as also the aptitude for the mission comes first of all from the Holy Spirit. The rôle of the hierarchy is, therefore, to "discern spirits", to set aside what does not come from the Holy Spirit, humbly to retain what appears to come from him and to supervise the harmony of everyone's actions. It knows in particular that "no one can be speaking through God's Spirit if he calls Jesus accursed, . . . it is only through the Holy Spirit that anyone can say Jesus is the Lord" (1 Cor. 12. 3). It also knows that the gift "which is better than any other" (1 Cor. 12. 31) is charity.

THE GIFTS OF THE HOLY SPIRIT

Although there is only one Gift of God, it is divided into a thousand different gifts and is applied in a thousand ways. Scripture attributes certain gifts to the Spirit of God, and the Church, moved by the very sure instinct of the Holy Spirit, recognizes in them those necessary qualities by virtue of which the children of God, having become docile to God through them, can act divinely. These are the gifts of the Holy Spirit.

Before presenting them, however, we must emphasize the unity of our spiritual organism.

The theological virtues (Faith, Hope and Charity), the gifts of the Holy Spirit (Understanding, Knowledge, Wisdom, Fear, Counsel, Piety, Fortitude), the moral virtues (Prudence, Justice, Fortitude and Temperance and all the virtues, which in their dependence on these four poles of orientation enable us to think and govern well, to will as the well-being of each and every one demands, to surmount courageously the obstacles which stand in the way of our good acts, to restrain the blind and excessive outbursts of certain passions, in short, to rule

[18] L. M. Dewailly, op. cit., p. 70.

suitably the whole sphere of our human life) are not separate or separable qualities. Whoever is a son of God by grace, possesses all these virtues and gifts. Whoever possesses one virtue under the influence of grace, attests thereby that he possesses them all. We are either living or not living. The life of the Holy Spirit in the soul takes care of this organic structure of stable dispositions which correspond to our various modes of action. In this regard, all the faithful possess all the gifts, even if it is also true that not everyone possesses them all equally. It is in this sense that a saint, for example, is said to possess the gift of counsel, not that he does not possess all the others, but that he has the privilege of possessing this gift pre-eminently.

Everything is contained implicitly in a living faith, in the faith of one who clings to God with his whole being in view of the Kingdom and who lives in charity with his neighbour. Or, to put it another way, all is contained in that love which puts the seal on faith and gives it its life.

But faith and charity do not in themselves convey the various dispositions of which they are capable. So it is a step forward for theology to take stock of these latter and, in so doing, to show the manifold exigencies in every sphere of the believing soul in quest of a more perfect love. The gifts express love's need of docility. He who loves is docile. He is ever disposed to welcome the words of the one he loves, to conform to his good pleasure, to receive all help from him, and that in a natural and spontaneous manner. Discovering the existence of these gifts is at the very heart of the fundamental Christian experience in which a certain spiritual instinct makes us grasp more directly and surely the good towards which God leads us than does the very simple reasonings of a soul pardoned by God and only anxious to do good. We notice, then, that "there is a gap between the theological virtues and the spontaneity needed for a participation in the divine life, not because the virtues are inadequate but because we are unable to take full advantage of them without the promptings of the Holy Spirit—those supremely subtle, swift and freely-given promptings of which the rigid practice of virtue in this world takes no account. The logical demonstration of this would be laborious, but in the intimate understanding which experience brings we can gain a full and harmonious insight into the laws of the perfection of grace."[19]

The gifts are then inferior to the theological virtues which in some way contain them. They express certain of their virtualities. But they are superior to all the moral virtues. They express that most noble quality of the soul which, beyond what it sees, what it knows itself capable of, and can adjust, takes as its supreme rule of action docility to God, in allowing God to lead it where he pleases. The gifts express this truth of our faith, that the saint is not only one who is fortified with virtuous dynamisms, but one who is completely in the hands of God, easily and promptly alive to God's least inspirations and desires. In this way the gifts represent something peculiar to theology, something the philosophers never knew. But what other way is there to express this necessary pliability of the spiritual bow in the hands of the divine Artist who wants to draw forth music?

Yet, comparison is not reason. Let us not think that the gifts are purely passive qualities. The words which we use, having been conceived for material movement, are to some extent unsuitable for the sphere to which we apply them. What moves the spirit save the spirit itself? In being moved by the Spirit of God, the spirit does not cease to move itself as well. Let us say that, through the gifts, it receives the grace to move itself freely, joyously and graciously, smoothly and without any resistance, in the exact line in which God wills it to move.

Christian tradition, marvellously understanding, through the Holy Spirit who sustains it, has preserved from the riches of God the list of the seven gifts which Isaias recognized in the Messias. Theology has seen a connection between the gifts and virtues, each gift being particularly linked with a virtue in order to perfect it and bring it to completion, by adjusting it perfectly to the

[19] M. D. Chenu, O.P., *Is Theology a Science?* Volume 2 in this series, p. 66.

hand of God who inspires or moves it. Thus the gift of understanding ministers to faith; it makes it more lucid and intelligible and particularly sensitive to recognizing God's action in
every event. The gift of knowledge corresponds to hope;
through it, the mind forms a judgement on perishable goods
and guards itself against placing in them too great and im-
moderate a confidence in relation to what it gives God. The
gift of wisdom corresponds to charity. It helps in the apprecia-
tion of divine love and the experience of God's sweetness and
kindness which it renders particularly perceptible. The gift of
counsel, midway between the gifts of reflection and the gifts of
action, is necessary for the truly prudent man whom it shows
all the principles involved in good actions. The gift of piety is
the ornament of all justice, especially that eminent justice
which is the virtue of religion; before rendering to God the
worship due to him, it inclines us to love what is due. The gift
of fortitude makes the soul so attached to God that it joyously
overcomes every obstacle. Finally, the gift of fear corresponds
with temperance since he who keeps his heart always humbly
submissive to the majesty of God is less liable to permit himself
to be carried away surreptitiously by the movement of an evil
passion.

But beyond this necessary specialization, we must remember
that the gifts cause a fresh, pure stream to flow into the soul, by
virtue of which what was dead or sickly comes to life again,
what was worn, becomes new again, and what was rigid,
supple. That is what is signified by the "fruits of the Holy
Spirit" which theology has taken from the reading of St Paul.[20]
Like a good breeze in springtime which, wherever it blows,
makes the land spring to life, so the Holy Spirit brings forth
fruit wherever he penetrates among the hearts of men.

Going beyond the gifts and the fruits, we may note that
everywhere in Scripture as in the liturgy and its teaching, the
Church, throughout her long tradition, attributes uprightness
of heart, liberty, gaiety, the joy of a tender love, freshness of

[20] Cf. Gal. 5. 22–23; Ephes. 5. 9; Philipp. 1. 11; 4. 17; 1 Cor. 13, 47.

spiritual sentiments and the gentleness of a good and compassionate heart, to the Holy Spirit. Perfection is made easy. This supreme ease, this joyous expansion in virtue, even in what is difficult, but beyond the deliberations of discursive reasoning, is the work of the Holy Spirit.

When the wind of the Spirit blows, the soul, guided by the gifts, is like a boat under sail which a very sure wind drives straight towards its port.

Let us reflect once again on this comparison. It should not make us misunderstand the virtues which, like the navigators' oars, often demand a definite effort. We do not appreciate the gifts and know them better by depreciating the virtues. Both have their own work which differentiates them. That of the gifts is to make the soul docile, supple, readily and joyously malleable in the hands of the Sovereign Master. By making the soul fully aware of its profound calling, this ability of being readily alive to every manifest will of God hallows its joy. *Gaudium de Veritate.* Joy is undoubtedly the final expression of the gifts and of the Holy Spirit.

Because he completes the work of Christ, which in turn completes the work of creation, the final note of the Spirit is a note of joyfulness. The Holy Spirit is the joy of the Church and the soul. We said that he was a "weight" in the heart of the Father and the Son, but a weight which draws and carries them towards each other in a transport of happiness. A similar weight draws the heart of this Spouse, the Church, towards the Son with whom the covenant has been sealed in the blood of the cross. It is a weight which makes all flesh that bears it active. Wherever the Spirit is, there generally arises, along with a deeper faith and adherence to Christ, the expansion of the heart and a joy that inspires the expression of gratitude.

CHAPTER VII

THE MISSION OF THE HOLY SPIRIT

"To prove that you are sons", writes St Paul, "God has sent out the Spirit of his Son into your hearts, crying out in us, Abba, Father" (Gal. 4. 6). "This is our proof that he is really dwelling in us, through the gift of his Spirit" (1 John 3. 24; cf. 4. 13).

The sending or the gift of the Holy Spirit is the goal of God's plan, the purpose towards which he has ordered everything. Salvation consists in accepting the Spirit, becoming the host, the Temple or property of the Spirit, and then in walking according to the Spirit of God: "A man cannot belong to Christ unless he has the Spirit of Christ" (Rom. 8. 9). "Surely you know that your bodies are the shrines of the Holy Spirit, who dwells in you. And he is God's gift to you, so that you are no longer your own masters" (1 Cor. 6. 19; cf. 1 Cor. 3. 16; Rom. 5. 5; John 14. 17). The Spirit, once he has taken possession of the Christian, anoints him, "marks him with his seal", confers on him "a foretaste" of the heavenly heritage (2 Cor. 1. 21–22), and gathers him with all his brethren into the unity of the Father and the Son (1 John 17. 21).

The sending of the Spirit is so necessary for our salvation that Jesus said to his apostles before leaving them: "And yet I can truly say that it is better for you I should go away; he who is to befriend you will not come to you unless I do go, but if only I make my way there, I will send him to you" (John 16. 7).

What, therefore, does this "sending", this "gift", this "dwelling" of the Holy Spirit in us, mean? Of course, Christ's promise can also refer to the visible sending of the Holy Spirit upon the apostles on the day of Pentecost. But the passages which we have just quoted show that this manifestation of the Spirit has meaning only in relation to what is interiorly bestowed upon the apostles on that solemn day. Therefore, we shall try to understand this visible mission as a consequence of the invisible mission which it manifests and which we consider in the first place.

THE MEANING OF SENDING

How can a divine person be "sent"? God is everywhere. St Augustine asks:

> Where can he who mightily reaches from one end of the earth to the other and sweetly disposes all things, be without his Word and his Wisdom? Can he be somewhere without his Spirit? If God is everywhere, his Spirit is everywhere. Consequently, the Spirit is sent where he was. And if the Son and the Spirit are sent where they were, we must try to understand what this mission of the Son and the Holy Spirit is meant to imply.[1]

The Holy Spirit is sent where he was already dwelling, is given where he was already possessed; he begins to dwell where he has been for all time. While we are striving to understand this special *mission* of the Holy Spirit, we must at the same time rigorously defend the inseparability of the Persons, their reciprocal interpenetration, without which our God would no longer be the one God of our faith. Leo XIII wrote:

> There is danger in faith or worship of confounding the three divine Persons among themselves or of dividing their unique nature; for Catholic faith venerates one God in Trinity, and Trinity in Unity. Therefore, Innocent XIII, our predecessor, flatly refused, despite earnest requests, to authorize a special feast in honour of the Father. For although we celebrate particular mysteries of the Word Incarnate, there is, nevertheless, no feast which

[1] *De Trinitate*, 2, Chapters 7 and 8.

honours the human nature as such, and the solemnities of Pentecost were established in the earliest times not simply for honouring the Holy Spirit in himself, but to commemorate his descent, that is, his visible mission. . . . In prayers addressed to one of the three Persons, mention is made of the others; in the litanies, a common invocation accompanies the invocation that is addressed separately to each of the three Persons. In psalms and hymns the same praise is addressed to the Father, the Son and the Holy Spirit; blessings, sacred rites, the sacraments, are either accompanied or followed by a prayer to the Holy Trinity.[2]

We must, therefore, understand the mission of the Holy Spirit in such a way that the word keeps its significance and yet does not indicate any separation of the Persons nor any change in God, since that is impossible.

Moreover, this is not a unique instance. When we say that God creates or produces such and such an effect, that he rewards or punishes or sends his prophets, we must also understand it in such a way that it does not involve any change of act or sentiment in God. "In me, the Eternal, there is no change" (Malachias 3. 6).

However, the divine mission leads us to consider God not only in his relation to creatures but in his inmost trinitarian relations. There seems to be a dialogue between the Persons at the term of which the Father and the Son send or give the Holy Spirit. Theology strives to enter into this divine conversation.

What, therefore, do we mean when we speak of a mission or sending? A mission is given to someone when he is sent to someone else or to something, to fulfil a certain rôle. Hence, a mission implies a twofold relationship: one to the sender, on whom the sending depends, and the other to the end or term to which he is sent.

The Sender

In human relations we can give a mission or send either as a leader, as for example when a master sends a servant, or as a

---

[2] Encyclical, *Divinum Illud Munus*, May 9th, 1897.

counsellor, as when we say that the king's adviser sends him to war by urging him to do so. But none of these sendings can be compared with the relations of the divine Persons, since they are equals. There is neither leader nor adviser among them. Yet, there is an order of origin. The Father is neither the Son nor the Holy Spirit. So we can speak of mission or sending just as we speak of procession without thereby implying some difference in dignity. In somewhat the same way we say that the flower "sends forth" its perfume. Considered on the side of the sender, the mission is identical with the procession. Each Person who proceeds can, by that fact, be sent.

The term of the sending: contact with God

But the mission does not consist solely in departing or "going out from". We depart for something. It is the same as when we say that we "have a mission".

Now, it is true that neither the Son nor the Spirit can be sent where they are not already, since both are God. Wherever a place exists, no matter where it is, it is God, Father, Son and Holy Spirit, who has created it and gives it its status as this place. But there need not be a displacement of the Person sent for there to be a mission. Is not a bishop sometimes named legate or representative by the pope to his own diocese? Without having to change his residence, he enjoys a new authority where he is; the diocese receives him no longer simply as bishop but as legate. So, the Son and the Spirit can be sent to a creature without any movement on the part of the Son or the Spirit—which would be meaningless—but by reason of a certain modification in the relationship which unites the creature to God.

What, therefore, is this modification? How can God be in his creature in a new manner? Is not God already everywhere, as the old adage says, "by his power", just as a king is in his whole kingdom, "by his presence", in the sense that everything is under his gaze, "by his essence", in the sense that his very being fills everything that exists? That is true. But if every being is under God's power and gaze, and is bound to and dependent on God in its very existence, not every being has the privilege of touching God and reaching him in the way he can be reached, that is, by naming him, knowing, loving and embracing him spiritually, as it were. Spiritual creatures alone are capable of that. But only grace can give them the power to turn towards him who created them in his Wisdom and Love, to attain him in himself through his Love and Wisdom. Contact, therefore, is established between God and his creature. God, who beheld his creature, can be seen as he is in himself and in his intentions by one who was unaware of him. A friend can appear from what was only, so to say, a sleeping creature. The "I" of God can raise up before him someone who says "thou" to him, a possible speaker who may also be an "I" to whom God can speak, by whom he can be understood, whom he can draw to himself.

The divine mission consists in this gift of grace which qualifies the spiritual creature to touch God no longer simply as the effect, unknowingly, "touches" the supreme Cause whence it comes and which touches it much more than it touches the cause, not only as the philosopher "touches" the causality of being at the term of his analysis, not knowing that this latter is Someone, nor who this Someone is, but touching God in himself, by a knowledge that "breathes love". To attain him in any other way is to remain far from him. Only the gift of grace can enable us to grasp in some sort, in its secret and intimacy, the uncreated Gift for which God has made us. St Thomas writes:

> Other creatures resemble the God who creates, conserves and moves them, but they do not attain God in his very person. So, although God is in them, they themselves are not with God. But the rational creature attains God himself through grace by knowing and loving him; we even say that it is with him. For this very reason we say that it has a capacity for God, that is, a capacity for the good which will perfect it as its Object. Therefore, we call the rational creature the Temple of God, the dwelling place of God.[3]

[3] I *Sentences*, Dist. 37, Exposition.

Thus defined, the divine mission does not introduce any change into God. However, the mission does inaugurate something; and since this is not in God, it can only be in the soul which is visited or dwelt in by the three divine Persons "sent". To say that these latter dwell in us or that we receive or possess them is to say that they transform us, that they enlighten our understanding, enkindle our heart, imprint in us the traits of their likeness. "But all those who did welcome him", says St John, "he empowered to become children of God" (John 1. 12). In the same way, God is not changed in his sentiments when he "pardons" or "endows with grace"; it is the soul that is changed by effective pardon or by the grace of God, and from a rebel becomes a willing servant and a friend. The divine mission adds to the word "procession" the fact that an event has taken place in the world: Jesus, the Church or a soul have been touched by God in such a way that they have an entirely new contact with God; but God himself is in no way changed.

It is for this reason that a mission constitutes a "real relation" of the spiritual creature to God and only a "logical relation" of God to the creature. This means that God is not affected in himself by this renewal in the creature, no more than he is affected in himself by the fact of creating or producing outside himself. Besides, what does "outside" of God mean? Can there be an outside and an inside, a before and an after for him? The fact that new creatures exist does not really confer new relations on him as it does on a creature, when, for example, a father "has" a new child or when someone "makes" a new acquaintance. The mystery is in the way in which creatures are bound up with their Cause and permeated by it, unable to be outside it and yet infinitely distinct from it. God is not affected by these temporal missions of the Word and the Spirit, whose cause and reason are the eternal processions. As for those who are visited by the Spirit or the Son, not only "have" they a new relation to God, but they are transformed by this very relation which they could not attain of themselves.

By Love, they enter into communion with the Son in the bosom of the Father.

THE IMAGE OF GOD IN THE SOUL

This last formula sets us on the road to further preciseness. We said that the divine missions change our soul, placing in it the mark of the Persons who are sent, and thus we can know God and love him as he knows and loves himself. The missions of the divine Persons communicate to us the very likeness of these Persons.

> Because the Holy Spirit is Love, it is the gift of charity that makes our soul resemble the Holy Spirit, and it is by reason of charity that we consider a special mission of the Holy Spirit. As for the Son who is the Word, not just any word but he who breathes Love, he whom St Augustine tried to define by calling him "an understanding full of love", his mission does not consist in perfecting in some way the understanding but in instructing it in such a way that it forthwith surrenders itself to the affections of love. Thus it is written: "Everyone who listens to the Father and learns, comes to me" (John 6. 45). And again, "In my meditation a fire shall flame out" (Ps. 38. 4, Douay Version). St Augustine explicitly says: "The Son is sent when he is known and in some sort perceived." The word perception implies a certain experimental or affective knowledge. It is what we properly call the wisdom (*sapientia*) that is a sweet (*sapida*) knowledge.[4]

The divine missions, by infusing in us this sweet knowledge and love which are appropriated to the Word and the Spirit, make our souls an image of God.

We should, however, give special attention to this beautiful and important word: the *image* of God. It forms part of our theological and even "spiritual" vocabulary; then it is fundamental in the Bible and remains so in the thought and piety of our forebears in the faith.

To begin with, the image is not a "vestige". Image implies a

[4] *Summa Theol.* Ia, qu. 43, art. 5, ad 2.

divine nature" and enables us to enjoy the presence of the divine Persons in us. It is in this sense that the Holy Spirit is said to have dwelt among the just of the Old Covenant although the final mission of the Holy Spirit, destined to make them enter into glory, had been retarded until the death of Christ and his descent into hell.

SPECIAL MISSIONS

But may we not imagine new missions of the Spirit during the time in which a holy soul, filled with the Holy Spirit and in this way re-created in the image of God, preserves itself from any sin that would exclude the gift of sanctifying grace? We can certainly do so provided there corresponds with each new mission a certain renewal in the soul.

This renewal can be understood in two ways, either as an extension of grace to a new sphere or as an increase in the intensity and fervour of grace. Grace is extended to a new sphere when it gives someone, for example, the power of working a miracle, of speaking in tongues or the gift of prophecy. There is, then, in each of these instances a new mission. There is an increase of grace when by the signal fervour of charity we accept martyrdom or even enter religion or undertake a difficult pilgrimage.[6] This does not mean that there is a new mission with every act of charity, but only at the moment of this most fervent act which in some way surpasses the measure of grace already possessed and corresponds to an increase of the gift of God. When God touches a soul to make it live, this cannot be without a vital reaction in this soul. There is a connection between each divine mission in a soul and the intense act of charity which, at a given moment, goes beyond the former possibilities of this soul. This act can be expressed in contemplation or prayer, in fraternal charity or in any virtue whatever.

Even though certain modern treatises consider more in detail

[6] These examples were inspired by St Thomas, *Summa Theol.* Ia, qu. 43, art. 6, ad 2.

conclusive resemblance, such, for example, as the same pare
age or family confers. We say that a son is the image of
father; we do not say that a house is the image of the archite
—except perhaps in a metaphorical sense. Thus we reserve t
name, image of God, who is spirit, for spiritual creature
In irrational creatures we do not find the image but only
"vestige" of God.

Secondly, God is living. The image of God must be too. Go
is living. His life, though it is immanent, is not less a life: a
eternal act of knowledge and love. The image of God shines i
us when we truly live, that is, when we know and love God a
he knows and loves himself.

Hence, there are degrees in the image of God. The image i
perfect among the blessed who, by the gift of glory, see Goc
face to face as the Son sees him and embraces him through the
Spirit who draws him in love. The image of God is discernible,
although to a lesser degree, in him who knows and loves, even
if still imperfectly, through conformity with grace, either because he possesses the *habitus* of these acts of knowledge and
love, that is, has been enabled to produce them although he
does not yet produce them, or at least not constantly. A good
example of this is the baptized infant who has received the
capacity for knowing and loving God although it is as yet unable to bring forth these acts because of an undeveloped intel-
ligence. It is the same with a child of God who is sleeping.
Finally, in a still lesser degree, the image of God is found in
every man who, although he has not received the gift of grace
or has refused it, possesses in himself, nevertheless, by his
nature a certain aptitude[5] for knowing and loving God.

We also say that there is a new mission and indwelling when
man passes from the image by natural aptitude to the image by
conformity with glory.

The indwelling of the Holy Spirit corresponds, then, to the
gift of sanctifying grace which renders us "participators of the

[5] *Secundum quod homo habet aptitudinem naturalem ad intelligendum et
amandum Deum* (*Summa Theol.* Ia, qu. 93, art. 4, c).

the "mystery" of man than directly the mystery of God in the
intimacy of the Persons, this is not the place to study the
"graces of prayer" or those of progress in virtue. We simply
observe that this renewal of the gift of God is not perceptible
to the senses. The Person sent makes himself known by a new
likeness or fullness which he gives the one in whom he comes to
dwell; but this likeness is not "sensible"—apart from the
special revelation which certain visible missions produce—
except through signs. It is thus that the apostles were able to
recognize "men . . . full of the Holy Spirit" (Acts 6. 3). A very
sure instinct for the Holy Spirit guided them as it often guides
the saints. But this "instinct" is quite other than self-confidence
since it is also permeated with the fear of God, with the fear of
straying from truth and humility. No one can boast that he
possesses the Holy Spirit and his divine instinct. This knowledge through signs is, therefore, never a clear and direct
knowledge, there is always the possibility of mistake. Yet, it is
sufficient for action in each case or giving advice when it is
requested.

In certain cases, however, the invisible mission is manifested
and gives place to what we call a visible mission. We have an
example of this in the mission or sending of the Holy Spirit,
under the form of a dove, to the Jordan at the moment of
Jesus' baptism. Similarly Jesus' last breath (John 19.30), which
served as a prelude to the outpouring of the Holy Spirit upon
the apostles (John 20. 22), was another instance. So also is the
descent of the Holy Spirit at Pentecost. St Thomas writes:

> In the invisible mission of the Holy Spirit, grace is poured into
> the soul from the fullness of divine love; and through this working
> of grace, the subject to whom the mission is directed receives an
> experimental knowledge of the divine Person. It is the same with a
> visible mission; there is an outpouring, but on another plane:
> again, because of a fullness, interior grace flows forth abundantly
> in its manner in a visible manifestation in which the indwelling of
> the divine Person is manifested not only to the subject but to
> others as well. Therefore, two conditions are required for a visible

mission: there must be a fullness of grace in the subject of the
mission, and what is more, this fullness must be ordered to others,
that is, this superabundant grace must flow forth in some manner
upon others. Thus, this visible mission was first made to Christ and
then to the apostles. It is through them that the Church has been
planted . . . in the universal diffusion of the knowledge of God.[7]

We can, although in a less strict sense, enlarge the notion of
"visible mission" as St Thomas understands it, by using it for
every manifestation of the Spirit intended for the benefit of all.
Such are the particular gifts and charisms distributed by the
Spirit of God to the different members of the Church for the
common good (1 Cor. 12. 4–11), at least where these gifts are
planted in souls which are themselves "filled with the Holy
Spirit". Such, in particular, is the gift of "prophecy" or preaching which the Spirit gives to certain missionaries whom he sends
forth to new lands and peoples that the Church might be
planted everywhere.[8]

The early Christian community was conscious of living under
the Breath of God. A limited and exceptional instance? Yes,
indeed, since the Church had to be founded absolutely. But in
the divine economy, the manifestations of the Breath are the
first fruits of every mission. "With plain evidence of the Spirit
and of power" (2 Cor. 2. 4, Westminster Version), that is what
missionary preaching is at all times, even if the word of the
preacher is without "pretensions to eloquence" (1 Cor. 2. 1). A
"mission" is a "breath" which passes over a people as the
breath over a visible harp, to move the inner and secret chords
of the soul which God has placed there in view of that harmony
which is assent of faith. That is why the mission must begin in

[7] I *Sentences*, Dist. 16, qu. 1, art. 2.

[8] St Thomas asked himself: Should not the Blessed Virgin, who had
the greatest fullness of grace ever given to a creature, also have been
permitted a visible mission? He then answered: "She has a share in the
mission at Pentecost with the first fruits of the Church. As for a special
visible mission, her grace did not demand it since she was not, like the
apostles, charged with planting the Church by preaching doctrine or
administering the sacraments." Cf. I *Sentences*, Dist. 16, qu. 1, art. 2,
ad 4.

the very life and work and activity of the people, as an inspired breath which is in some way secretly awaited by them. The missionary does not have to bring his own orchestra and provide all the music—all his theology—but first of all listen for the fundamental note on which all the chords of the people and their souls vibrate, that of the Love of God, manifested in the death and resurrection of his Son. The mission is, in the first place, like a breath of springtime which awakens the sleeping earth and makes life spring forth. The elaboration of belief, the imposition of signs and various ministerial functions of the Church come logically, if not in order of time, later. We order and improve only what already lives.

CHAPTER VIII

THE LAW OF THE SPIRIT
AND FREEDOM

"Where the Lord's Spirit is, there is freedom" (2 Cor. 3. 17).

Throughout its history, from the Exodus to the time of Christ, Israel was repeatedly abandoning Yahweh. But however great this desertion and forgetfulness of Yahweh, God did not abandon his people. The prophets foretold that the covenant, the law and its promulgation were to be renewed on a deeper level. In the prophetic vision on the promulgation of the law Mount Sion at Jerusalem was seen gradually to supplant Mount Sinai "which is in Arabia" (Gal. 4. 25):

> This is a message which was revealed to Isaias, the son of Amos, about Juda and Jerusalem. In later days the mountain where the Lord dwells will be lifted high above the mountain-tops, looking down over the hills, and all nations will flock there together. A multitude of peoples will make their way to it, crying, Come, let us climb up to the Lord's mountain-peak, to the house where the God of Jacob dwells; he shall teach us the right way, we will walk in the paths he has chosen. The Lord's commands will go out from Sion, his word from Jerusalem. (Isaias 2. 1–3.)

The true Sinai, or at least the mountain of the true covenant and the definitive Law, is Mount Sion at Jerusalem. Is there not an element of prophecy in the fact that the old law, which had been forgotten, was found on Sion (4 Kings 22–23)? Already in Psalm 98 Moses and Aaron are seen on Mount Sion speaking with Yahweh "in the pillar of cloud" and receiving the Law.

Another Psalm (14) presents a new decalogue as coming from Sion.

Therefore, it is at Jerusalem that the disciples must stay to await "the Father's promise", the realization of the covenant. The theophany on Sinai is made present again in the Cenacle at Jerusalem: "All at once a sound came from heaven like that of a strong wind blowing" (Acts 2. 2; cf. Exodus 19. 16), to stress the continuity of these two events, or at least to show the significance of the second event. The apostles appeared with "what seemed to be tongues of fire" (Acts 2. 3), just as Moses and Aaron had seen "the whole of Mount Sinai ... wreathed in smoke, where the Lord had come down with fire about him" (Exod. 19. 18). The feast of Pentecost, which was the harvest-feast (Exod. 34. 22; Deut. 16. 9) as well as the feast of the promulgation of the Law on Sinai, became the feast for the descent of the Spirit at Jerusalem. The gift of an inner law, that of the Spirit, renews the gift of the external law. Thus St Paul was able to write to the Corinthians that his letter of recommendation, that which makes him acceptable to them, is themselves, a letter from Christ "written not in ink, but in the Spirit of the living God, with human hearts, instead of stone, to carry it" (2 Cor. 3. 3).

TWO ECONOMIES

Since the Law proved itself unable to bring forth justice (that is, salvation or holiness), it was henceforth void. "You, who look to the law for your justification, have cancelled your bond with Christ, you have forfeited grace. All our hope of justification lies in the Spirit" (Gal. 5. 4–5). Why return to the Law, why impose it upon the pagan if it is unable to justify us? "Stand fast and do not let yourselves be caught again in the yoke of slavery. The word of Paul is your warrant for this; if you are for being circumcised, Christ is of no value to you at all" (Gal. 5. 1–2).

The old antagonism discerned at the beginning of biblical

history between "the flesh", the earthly principle, and the breath, the principle of the life which comes from above, here assumes its full meaning, its final and definitive significance: "Learn to live and move in the spirit, then there is no danger of your giving way to the impulses of corrupt nature. The impulses of nature and the impulses of the spirit are at war with one another; either is clean contrary to the other, and that is why you cannot do all that your will approves" (Gal. 5. 16–17).

Since the Law was not yet penetrated by the Spirit, the regime of the Law was still an economy of the flesh; and since it was powerless of itself to sanctify, it was in fact verified as an economy of sin and death (Rom. 8. 7). But then the Spirit came. "It is by letting the spirit lead you that you free yourselves from the yoke of the law" (Gal. 5. 18). "The spiritual principle of life has set me free, in Christ Jesus, from the principal of sin and death . . . but you live the life of the spirit, not the life of nature; that is, if the Spirit of God dwells in you. A man cannot belong to Christ unless he has the Spirit of Christ" (Rom. 8. 2, 9). Salvation comes to us, not from the law but from the Spirit who begets faith in our souls. "Now we are quit of the claim which death had on us, so that we can do service in a new manner according to the spirit, not according to the letter as of old" (Rom. 7. 6).

For St Paul, this doctrine is central. He becomes very angry directly it is challenged. He is not afraid to denounce to the Galatians "those false brethren who insinuated themselves into our company so as to spy on the liberty which we enjoy in Christ Jesus" (2. 4). And unable to shout out to them what he has to tell them—their call to liberty—he makes his writing larger: "Here is some bold lettering for you, written in my own hand" (Gal. 6. 11).

No doubt the Law from which the Galatians and Romans are delivered is the Mosaic law, in which the Jews put their trust (Rom. 2. 17). It is with it, then, that we are concerned in these Epistles. But it suffices to re-read these latter to realize what St Paul is aiming at farther on. As Fr Lyonnet, S.J., professor at the Pontifical Biblical Institute in Rome, so rightly says, "These statements concerning the Mosaic law, not considered as Mosaic but simply as law, apply in fact to every law which is imposed on man from without".[1] Further on, in Romans 7, St Paul seems "to evoke not only the transgression of the Jews against the Mosaic law, but still more the disobedience of Adam in the earthly paradise, the type of all others".[2] To present their call to liberty only in relation to the old Mosaic law and flagrantly to weigh them down with precepts and new commands when they are truly delivered from every "regime of law" would be an imposition on Christians. The economy of the Mosaic law was the type and symbol of every economy of law. It was sufficient for the apostles, once they had received the Spirit, and for all the circumcised believers who had come with Peter to the home of the centurion, Cornelius, at Caesarea to realize "that the free gift of the Holy Spirit could be lavished upon the Gentiles" (Acts 10. 45), in order to understand that henceforth "man is justified by faith apart from the observances of the law" (Rom. 3. 28). There is only one God "who will justify the circumcised man if he learns to believe, and the Gentile because he believes" (Rom. 3. 30).

However, the law was not useless. It "was our tutor, bringing us to Christ, to find in faith our justification" (Gal. 3. 24). Henceforth, faith confers on the law all its value (cf. Rom. 3. 31), since faith alone allows it to attain its end which is the justice and holiness of man (Rom. 7. 7). But it is faith and not the external practice of the law that confers justice. Thus St Paul can write in one of those paradoxical formulas of which he was so fond, that "the law of faith" frees us from the practice of the law (cf. Rom. 3. 27).

Let us grasp what this means. The fact that the economy of

---

[1] S. Lyonnet, *Les Epîtres de saint Paul aux Galates et aux Romains* (Paris, Ed. du Cerf, 1953), p. 58.
[2] Ibid.

the law is void does not mean that there are no longer laws for the Christian and that every licence is permissible for him. "Yes, brethren, freedom claimed you when you were called. Only do not let this freedom give a foothold to corrupt nature; you must be servants still, serving one another in a spirit of charity" (Gal. 5. 13; cf. 1 Peter 2. 16). And, moreover, did not our Saviour say: "Do not think that I have come to set aside the law and the prophets; I have not come to set them aside but to bring them to perfection" (Matt. 5. 17). The "law of free-dom" (James 2. 12) ought not to contradict the laws but funda-mentally agree with them. But how?

For St Paul the world is divided between two divine "econo-mies". On the one hand there is the economy or regime of the Law, that of the old covenant. The law was a tutor to instruct us in what is good and to send us on our way to Christ. But as for bestowing on us the ability to act well, it was powerless. In fact, the economy of the law discharged itself in defeat; its worth lies in the fact that it gave us a knowledge of sin (Rom. 7. 7), of our debt and our condemnation. And as for this debt, Christ "swept it out of the way by nailing it to the cross" (Col. 2. 14). All those deceive themselves who put their justice (that is, salvation) in "works" (Rom. 3. 27), namely, in external acts commanded by the law, or laws. Our justice is in our heart where God, who has given us his Spirit, dwells. This justice of the heart or faith is, indeed, normally expressed by certain "works" or external acts—so much so that St James can ex-claim: "Show me this faith of thine without any deeds to prove it, and I am prepared, by my deeds, to prove my own faith" (James 2. 18)—but no one can pride himself on his deeds before God in order to be justified. If these have some worth, it is not in them that this worth is found before God, it is in the heart of him who accomplished them.

Thus, there is opposition between on the one hand the economy of the law, or of "works" or the letter, an economy which is in fact "carnal" and unable to acknowledge the Spirit, and on the other the economy of the new covenant, an economy of the Holy Spirit, who sanctifies man's heart, renews his inner being in a total adherence, which is the living faith, to God's plan as made manifest in Christ. It is an economy of faith (Rom. 3. 27), of grace (John 1. 17), of truth (John 8. 32) and of freedom in the Holy Spirit.

Even now let us make it clear that these two economies are not necessarily separated by the temporal demarcation of the Incarnation. "In all ages", says St Thomas, "there have been men belonging to the New Covenant."[3] He explains this by saying: "During the period of the covenant there were men with charity and grace from the Holy Spirit who awaited the spiritual and eternal promises. These already belonged to the new law."[4] Conversely, St Thomas shows that certain Christians "are still carnal" and that it is necessary "even during this period of the new covenant to lead them to acts of virtue through fear of penalties and through certain temporal promises"[5] which are proper to the old law, otherwise known as the law of fear or the law of constraint.

Enlarging on these statements St Thomas could write that the old law is every written law as such, every book, every writing considered as such, whereas the new law is the Holy Spirit who makes our hearts live by the very love of God. "The old law is a testament of the letter, but the New Testament is a testament of the Holy Spirit, through whom the love of God has been poured out in our hearts (Rom. 5. 5). And since the Holy Spirit placed in us the love of charity which is the fullness of the law, the New Testament is written, not in letters but in the Spirit who gives life (Rom. 8. 11)."[6] Also, when St Paul declares "the letter kills but the spirit gives life", "by letter", as St Augustine explains, "we must understand every writing that is external to man, even such moral precepts as are contained in the Gospel. That is why even the letter of

[3] *Summa Theol.* Ia, qu. 106, art. 3, ad 2; cf. qu. 107, art. 1, ad 2, ad 3.
[4] *Ibid.* qu. 107, art. 1, ad 2.
[5] *Ibid.*
[6] In his commentary on 2 Cor. 3. 6.

the Gospel would kill unless there was the inner presence of the healing grace of faith."[7] The law of the Christian is no longer without but within.

LAWS AND LIBERTY

And yet, there are laws even in the Church. There are still external precepts in the economy of the new covenant as in every human society. How obey these laws, how fulfil them without being "under the law"? Is there not an absolute antinomy between the two regimes: that of "laws" or "works" on one side and that "of the Holy Spirit" on the other? The external law tends to make its subjects *static* beings, all conformed to the same mould, that of the law. Do we not often distinguish one race from another according as they are under one or another kind of law, statute law or common law, Western law or the law of the Koran, French or Germanic law? The Holy Spirit, on the contrary, is a *dynamic* principle within us, who makes us live, hope, love and adhere to Christ. Under the regime of law the tendency is towards fixity of gestures and external acts, at least inasmuch as laws do not change. There are not thirty-six ways of obeying the law. As soon as we begin to disregard any custom which it regulates, we ordinarily also begin to extricate ourselves from the law, and the law *is* no longer. With the "law of grace" infused in us by the Holy Spirit it is otherwise; life and movement are primary; as soon as a thing no longer moves, there is no longer life, there is death.

In short, the tendency of the economy of law is to fix and at the same time make everything completely rigid. No doubt order and discipline are thereby secured, but sometimes at the cost of constraint in life; men of order, external discipline and authority are not always evangelical men. If order prevails and men no longer ask themselves questions then "the law" is fulfilled. On the contrary, the life-giving Spirit does not prevent man from asking himself questions. As he gropes his way into

[7] *Summa Theol.* Ia-IIae, qu. 106, art. 2, c.

the mystery should not man, like Jacob, contend with every proffered truth to test the strength of each and not allow himself to be conquered too easily by what is not sufficiently proved?

According as the stress is placed on the external law or on the life that is within, we are in fact led to two contrary tendencies. It frightens "men of order" and "of law" to speak of liberty and life. And in a sense they are right (cf. 1 Peter 2. 16). They multiply laws to ensure the perfection of acts without considering further that the perfection acquired can be merely external.

Let us not be "pharisees" in accusing the pharisees on this point; such a state of mind exists in all ages. A moralist, examining the question of "servile work" on Sunday as forbidden or permissible, writes: "Is it allowed to copy a text, accounts or musical scores, to use a typewriter, to duplicate, to print?" Further on he judges it legitimate to "print, embroider, crochet and knit", which made one commentator react, and rightly so: "Very well! So it would be permissible to knit and yet it is forbidden to sew. . . . For us moralists, to knit is artistic, to sew, plebeian."[8] And this same commentator adds, not without references, that subtle minds will even distinguish "knitting a pull-over as artistic work and knitting stockings as servile".[9] This is far from an economy of liberty in the Holy Spirit.

And yet we cannot suppress laws as some, though wrongly, would sometimes like to do. Liberty of the Spirit is not anarchy. Laws are necessary for all social life. Human relations involve adjustment. Traffic must be directed either to the left or the right of the road so that each may subsequently circulate freely. There must be a timetable for religious or secular ceremonies, so that the community can assemble. The order of lessons and rites at all religious functions must be determined. And so on. Thus the way is open to a multiplication of legal determina-

[8] Cf. in *Le Jour du Seigneur*, the contribution by Mgr. M. Michaud, "Les oeuvres serviles" (Paris, Ed. R. Laffont, 1948), p. 215.
[9] *Ibid.*

tions. Where do they stop? And how do we avoid compromising "the law of liberty"?

LAW OF LIFE AND WRITTEN LAWS

In order to understand this, we should note at the start that the word law has a twofold meaning. Using this twofold meaning, St Paul was able to oppose the law of faith to the law of works (Rom. 3. 27), and tells us how "the spiritual principle of life has set me free in Christ Jesus, from the principle of sin and death" (Rom. 8. 2).

In a primary and fundamental sense law is a written proposition which regulates the actions of men and their relations. It is all the more perfect in itself according as its wording is clear and precise and does not suffer ambiguity. In that way it can be followed perfectly. The laws of the Old Testament concerning worship, ceremonies and judgements are laws of this type. So also are the laws in the various legal codes of the world, all statutes, constitutions, customs and precepts.

In a second and yet pre-eminent sense, the law is not to be understood as a grammatical proposition but as of a given nature. It is not just a construction of human reason but a divine institution, ordering and creating natures. Starting with the natures which he sees, man can strive to go back to the divine reason which instituted them, and thus discover the "laws" of these natures; but no logical proposition, not even a multitude of propositions can adequately explain a living nature. Many propositions can explain the law of respiration, blood circulation, generation etc., but none, not even all of them together, is sufficient to solve the unique mystery of this man who stands before me and is called Peter. We see Peter, but the unique "idea" or rather the word which expresses the mystery of Peter, of his being and life, is in God.

Even if he is unable to express it completely, man cannot go against the idea, the word or "law" that is in God. The "natural law", even if it cannot be formulated, governs, in a certain way, all laws. No law would have the force of law if it went against the "natural law". No man could legitimately legislate against it. No decree, even of the greatest monarch, could make moral what is by nature immoral. No law authorizing murder, for example, can make murder moral; such a law is not really legal. Hence, the natural law, although it can scarcely be called a law since it cannot be formulated, is the hidden basis of all laws. Even if it does not fall upon the ears like the words of a leader, it does set the norm for man. It is in this sense that the Holy Spirit infuses in us a "new law" which is in some way innate. St Thomas says "a thing is innate in man in either of two ways: in the sense that it concerns the nature of man, and it is thus that the natural law is innate in man, or in the sense that it is superadded to nature by the gift of grace; it is thus that the law of grace is innate in man, not only as indicating what he must do, but also helping him to accomplish it."[10]

Although law can have two different meanings, these two meanings are not unrelated. No written law can go against the natural law, and, *a fortiori*, against the law of grace. Conversely, the natural law, like the law of grace, lends itself to the establishment of numerous laws which strive at least partially to express it or to provide a background which enables man to fulfil himself or teaches him the way in which God, in his eternal Thought, calls man to himself.

Christian liberty, which the Holy Spirit pours into our hearts, consists in assimilating in some way and "interiorizing" external laws in such a way that they cease being external laws to become an internal law, a living law, a law of the heart. All these expressions are synonymous and have the same meaning as law of faith (Rom. 3. 27), the law of love,[11] or the law of freedom (James 2. 12).[12]

[10] *Summa Theol.* Ia-IIae, qu. 106, art. 1, ad 2.

[11] "The new law which consists essentially in spiritual grace itself, infused into hearts, is called the Law of love" (*Summa Theol.* Ia-IIae, qu. 107, art. 1, ad 2).

[12] St Thomas also compares it with a saying in James 1. 25: "the law of perfect liberty", but the meaning is less certain. *Op. cit.* Ia-IIae, qu. 108, art. 1, ad 2.

An external law is necessary, for example, and in so far as it is possible, to compel the thief or the liar not to steal or lie any more. The fear of the law or the sanction attached to it will sometimes lead them to prefer honesty or loyalty to their vice. But for the upright and honest man, these laws are no longer necessary. The permanent desire for what is just and true is a guarantee of good conduct. Hence the adage: "laws are coercive for evil-doers, but for the good they are simply regulative." But what is true in the order of primary and moral precepts is equally true in every order of human relations. If it is necessary to learn the rules and customs when one enters a given society—a military unit, a school, a religious order— then each one ends by knowing these relational rules and can adjust himself to others and to the society by interiorizing these rules. In Christian society, for example, it is easy to understand the rules or customs, such as certain days of fast or certain liturgical seasons, the Friday abstinence, reception of the sacraments of Penance and Eucharist at least once a year, and so on. To go to Mass because it is commanded instead of striving to understand the precept is to live even now under the regime of external law, under the economy of the old covenant. Our faith in the resurrection of Jesus and in his apparitions "the day following the sabbath" opens our understanding and makes us want the Christian community to be entirely united on this day, as a bride waiting for the bridegroom "until he comes" (1 Cor. 11. 27).

But can we completely "interiorize" all laws? Is this not a rather utopian idea? Can we one day live entirely according to our heart, perfectly adjusted, if we can so speak, to God and others without reference to any rule outside us? Can this ideal "law of the Spirit", seen as totally excluding all written law, be realized here below?

In point of fact, this ideal is the goal towards which we must aim and which is realized in the heavenly Jerusalem. Therefore its perfect realization is eschatological. We shall take our first steps as free men on the new earth and under the new heavens of the risen humanity. The Holy Spirit will then have this power, being completely in each and everyone, of spontaneously reconciling us to each other by a divine instinct, without the need of any other rule. It will be rather like those trees and flowers which man has neither planted nor sown, but which he discovers on virgin soil and whose colours and forms are wonderfully harmonized. But the Church militant stands between the synagogue whence it comes and the heavenly Jerusalem whither it leads us. The better part of her is free and bestows upon us liberty from on high. But a part of her, like the synagogue, is made up of laws, precepts, external signs, which teach us about liberty, educate and lead us to it. When the Temple of God, the Church, is complete, then what is synagogical will come to an end, and laws, sacraments, symbols and signs will cease, rather as the scaffolding is taken away once a house is completed.

CHRISTIAN "INTERIORIZATION" AND ITS LIMITATIONS

However, between the old covenant society and Christian society, which is the Church, there is a difference in the use of laws.

The Church leads us to the final liberty of the children of God, of those whom St Paul calls "sons", for they are no longer under the law, they are free: "But when the fullness of time was come, God sent his Son, made of a woman, made under the law: that he might redeem them who were under the law; that we might receive the adoption of sons. . . . Therefore, he is not a servant but a son" (Gal. 4. 4–7, Douay). Those who have the "Spirit of the Son" (Gal. 4. 6) cannot be under the yoke of the law any more. Therefore, the Christian legislator ought to command only what is possible of "interiorization" for each individual as for each community at each stage of its progress. St Thomas Aquinas is very firm on this point. Along with St Augustine he speaks, and not without a certain humour, of certain legal additions which "burden the life of the faithful" and he denounces certain legislators who "weigh down our religion which the mercy of God willed to be free—consisting of well defined but few necessary sacraments and signs—with burdens fit for slaves; so much so that the condition of the Jews who were subject to legal prescriptions and not to human presumption, appears more tolerable".[13] The Christian legislator ought to bear in mind the precept of Proverbs (30. 33): "Blow thy nose lustily and blood shall flow at last," that is to say, according to the commentary of St Thomas,[14] that the law which condemns every possible evil risks compromising the little good of which certain men are capable. Even if laws are useful, they are not the only means of securing the welfare of those whom we instruct by them. The prayer of others, the emulation of the common life, the love with which we are loved, friendship, example, are often found to be precious aids for the grace of the Holy Spirit. Whence the advice a certain desert Father gave to an abbot who came for guidance in the governing of his monks: "Be an example for them and not a legislator."

It does not follow, it must be added, that the Christian can judge for himself what he may "interiorize" and what, in his judgement, he may not. Especially is this so in the spiritual order where we do not "sense" our own powers, and where the best we do is God's work. But nothing stops the subject from presenting his case, if that is necessary, to the one who makes the laws or orders the activities so that the burdens he can bear and "interiorize" may be better adapted to him if they are not so already. However, we only "interiorize" what we love. The primary disposition for being free in that liberty to which the inner gift of the Spirit disposes us is to love. We are free when we love. We are slaves when we are forced, even if the burden we have is trivial. Love forms the line of demarcation between the old and the new Law. The Holy Spirit is the Spirit of liberty and filial adoption because he is the Spirit of love.

[13] *Summa Theol.* Ia-IIae, qu. 107, art. 4, c.
[14] *Ibid.* Ia-IIae, qu. 96, art. 2, ad 2.

It remains true that the burden imposed by laws, circumstances of life and activities, despite recourse to authority and the effort of love, can be ill-proportioned to what we are yet capable of "interiorizing". Here again, it is not for the subject to judge for himself without authoritative and competent counsel.

The Christian knows that despite all his desires to attain perfect freedom and his efforts towards this end it is not to be found here below. An unequal portion of laws, excessive burdens, irksome or humiliating duties, lie heavy upon everyone. With the whole creation "full of expectancy" (Rom. 8. 19), we "groan in common travail" (Rom. 8. 22) until we all "share in the glorious freedom of God's sons" (Rom. 8. 21). What is essential has already been given us through the love of God poured into our hearts. Are prison, slavery and suffering, when these are mixed with love, still nothing but prison, slavery and suffering? And since what is essential has been given us through the Holy Spirit, "who will separate us from the love of Christ? Will affliction, or distress, or persecution, or hunger, or nakedness, or peril or the sword? . . . Yet in all this, we are conquerors through him who has granted us his love" (Rom. 8. 35–7). The "law of the Spirit" must dwell in us even to the point where it seems all liberty is taken away and where yet we are free in the Holy Spirit.

THE FREE MAN

Do not these examples prove, however, that liberty has other exigencies which we have still not considered? How, in fact, can we say to prisoners in concentration camps or those bowed down under the yoke of crushing toil, for whom tomorrow is an uncertainty, to the infirm and even to slaves where they are still to be found: "You are free in the Spirit", if we do nothing to free them, however little, from their "chains"? "Here is a brother, here is a sister, going naked, left without the means to secure their daily food; if one of you says to them, Go in peace, warm yourselves and take your fill, without providing for their bodily needs, of what use is it?" (James 2. 15–16).

No doubt we shall answer, Christian liberty is of another order, a transcendent order, since it is bestowed on us through the inner gift of the Holy Spirit. But this transcendent gift works an unceasing renewal of our whole nature and our whole being. It is not only the inmost part of our spirit that is called to be free, to the exclusion of all the rest, but our whole being, although this is always through the gift of the Holy Spirit. The Holy Spirit "renews the face of the earth", not only through the invisible gift of liberty which he places in each soul, but through all the consequences of this gift, indeed in the life of each man, his works, his leisure as in human relations and even the structure of society.

This last requirement is of particular importance. Since each person is at once a source and channel of human relations, no one is perfectly free unless all are. How, in fact, could the dialogue of a man more advanced in the way of liberty not be hindered by the servitude of an interlocutor who lacks his daily bread and is a victim of hunger or of someone who has not the least leisure for thinking, reflecting and praying, or of someone who even lacks the elementary knowledge that will set him free. We cannot advance on the paths of liberty as free-lancers or as isolated individuals, but as a body, the whole of humanity as one united in the Breath of the Holy Spirit.

The techniques of liberation are of little importance here. Faith need not give us these, even if it is an incentive towards their pursuit. But, by virtue of the gift made to him, the Christian must be a pioneer in the fight for the liberation of man. Even if liberation from sin is the fundamental liberation, and especially if it is since without it there would be no other true liberation, the Christian endeavour goes further and aims at complete human liberation which is the sign and witness of a higher liberty for which it does not give up hoping. Who knows if certain men have not heard the Spirit's call "to liberty" (Gal. 5. 13) through the sign of more humble liberations of which they have been the object: liberation from their unfair deal, the bestowal of liberating knowledge, the possibility for the leisure necessary to their cultural growth and human expansion? St Paul himself thinks so, even he who forbids baptized pagans to place themselves under the yoke of the Mosaic law.

There can be no doubt that this battle is full of risks, snares and sometimes ambiguities. Then, too, the Christian more than any other, for he is the son of God, the son of liberty, must know what he wants and what he does. He knows that his liberty is principally the effect of divine adoption through the gift of the Holy Spirit. He must take care not to confuse liberty with the idea he makes of it, or even that idea which well intentioned men make of it, and *a fortiori* with the idol which the world adores.

> He will be on his guard lest he refers to liberty too lightly; he will prefer to say that Christ has made man free. . . . How many times under the guise of liberty have we not dared to impose narrow ideas and to forbid what each free man had every right to look forward to. By this rejection of every abstract idea as intangible truth, we are reminded that absolute truth, total Love, proceeding from complete liberty, are in this God whom no one has seen save the Son and whom no one knows save he to whom the Son has revealed him. Between the liberty which we already have and the liberty which we have yet to attain Christ preserves a great infinity where the liberty of each day finds its meaning.[15]

Consequently, it will not be unprofitable to consider from another angle—that of man and his liberty—what we have said about the Gift of the Spirit, whose Law in us is life and liberty.

To be free is to do what we *will*, to be master of ourselves and our acts. But what in reality does *willing* mean? And, above all, what does "self" imply? "I find, then, this law when I wish to do what is excellent, namely, that what is evil lieth to my hand. I delight in the law of God after the inner man, but I behold another law in my members, warring against the law in my

---

[15] A.-J. Maydieu, *Catéchisme pour aujourd'hui* (Paris, Ed. du Cerf, 1954), p. 64.

mind and making me captive to the law of sin which is in my members" (Rom. 7. 21, Westminster Version). To what does this "I" refer—to the "mind" or "the members", or simply to what is below the mind? No doubt it is my whole being, body and soul, all my qualities, my whole make-up, but most especially my spirit. Man begins to be free when his spirit is free. Man is a slave when his spirit yields to "the law in his members".

The germ of liberty which the Holy Spirit has placed in our souls is the promise of exceedingly lofty and divine ambitions. For the child of God, to be free is not only to act according to the spirit without being fettered to what is inferior, it is to desire with a will that progressively imitates more and more or reproduces increasingly better and better the will of Christ who is the image of God. Free will for the sons of God is increasingly perfect submission to God, a desire for God, a will efficacious of good, a good that is essentially divine, towards all men. In this sense the stages of liberty are the very stages of our growth in grace. A free act gives access to a greater liberty. And so, conversely, the least surrender of liberty sometimes opens the door to more important surrenders. Drinking can be a free act. But if drinking in certain circumstances is not "reasonable", if reason permits itself to be conquered by something outside it, drinking can suppress even for a time the liberty which we have for performing a free act. In the same way, "to let oneself go", to accept such a situation even freely, is to surrender the liberty of being free and acting freely. The path of liberty is rough, especially of that divine liberty which has been allotted to us and allows no respite.

We see, in passing, how this liberty in the Holy Spirit is more exacting than the law. Conformity to the law involves a few acts, precisely those acts the law requires. However long they take, they do not take all our time, nor do they monopolize completely the heart of him who performs them. The Pharisee, satisfied with his "works", thinks he can glory in himself because he "fasts twice a week and gives a tenth of his earnings".

In spite of all this he is acquitting himself rather easily, for in the economy of the Holy Spirit the believer can never do so. It is his heart, and whether it is docile to the Gift of the Spirit, that counts, not his deeds. He can never just present himself to God with his arms full of the deeds he has performed, for no matter how excellent these deeds may be, they are of no value in the sight of God, save in relation to the heart. The doer of the law, on the contrary, has an armful of deeds and a confident attitude precisely by reason of these deeds which belong to him and by which he thinks himself justified before God. But the man who believes in the economy of the Holy Spirit has a poor opinion of himself. He has nothing to give that God has not given him the power to offer, and his very heart which alone could justify him he does not understand. We have at the most a very faint idea, and this only through certain signs, of the generosity of our faith and the fervour of our love. And, moreover, we know that the remedy for our imperfections will always be the same: to realize an even greater love. We are never free from loving. We are never finished becoming still freer in the Holy Spirit since here love and liberty in their deepest meaning go together.

Our liberty like our love is never perfect, the more so as it is still not very manifest. The manifestation of love may be of little significance, but it is quite otherwise with liberty. A liberty which is still unable to manifest itself is no liberty at all. With the growth of our inner liberty, whether in ourselves or in our relations with others, there normally corresponds an incoercible and gradual striving consisting of feelings and interior dispositions. The excessive constraint of laws and of minute and burdensome regulations are not for the man who is free, *a fortiori* for the man to whom God has given the Spirit of his Son who is a Spirit of liberty. The Christian needs laws to teach him the path of goodness, that perfect goodness which is heavenly beatitude. But they cannot be indefinitely multiplied without causing harm. The exact measure of laws to be imposed on the Christian is, as we saw, that measure of laws, rules or regulations which can and ought to be "interiorized" and thus cease to be "external laws". Thus and thus only can they serve as a true gateway to the liberty of the children of God.

What is true of written laws or external orders should also be applied to all that is in a certain way "outside" man's spirit: customs, which are basically unwritten laws, social protocol and convention, human relations: and even "within" the human being, a diseased mind, for example, can hamper one's expression and compromise the full flowering of liberty. Sin is an example of this, but we are not here directly concerned with it.

Social distinctions and conventions are necessary for man's life, education and instruction. Man cannot be born without a father or mother; likewise he needs his fellow men in order to learn and work. Each human society, on grounds peculiar to it, constitutes a privileged source of human culture. But on the other hand, such elementary societies as the family, the nation or fatherland, into whose traditions an individual is born and grows up, a man's profession... can all be some sort of idol and ultimately enslave one who is not merely, nor even principally, the child of his parents, the citizen of an earthly city, a member of a profession, but the son of God. The son of God inevitably accepts the laws, customs, social customs and human conventions of his family, country or profession. He cannot do otherwise without injury to himself and others. But the child of God has also a more noble origin; his liberty would be in danger if he did not look beyond these. Growth in liberty for the sons of God demands constant discernment between the exigencies of their family, country and the milieu they live in, and those of God. He who would sacrifice—even were it only in his judgement or opinion—his liberty and life to strangers for the sake of glory or to his own people simply for "tranquillity" of mind, would cease being free with that liberty God gave to his sons. One social group would cease to be free if it sacrificed for its own comfort and limited ideals what another social group or class had to offer it by way of education, human advancement and so forth. Constant discernment is needed here, one that is difficult to realize. Without it there can be no advance in that divine liberty which the Holy Spirit gives. Fortunately, the Holy Spirit equips us for this discernment. "Mere man with his natural gifts cannot take in the thoughts of God's Spirit. . . . Whereas the man who has spiritual gifts can scrutinize everything without being subject, himself, to any man's scrutiny" (1 Cor. 2. 14–15). This does not mean, however, that he can always dispense with the counsel and advice of certain people. The Spirit of God endows us with the spirit of humility and disposes us to seek advice there where he shows us that good advice is to be found.

Perhaps we can enlarge on what we have just said and include other more "interior" domains even though these are always outside the spirit itself. We have mentioned the human mind and all its illnesses and traumatic conditions which psychology discovers and which sometimes interfere very seriously with the free exercise of spiritual faculties. In this sphere as in others, faith does not suggest methods nor the Holy Spirit ready-made recipes. It is enough that Christ has called us to the freedom of the children of God.

In order to be free, the Christian will not fear knowing himself, as St Catherine of Siena very fervently recommends in her apologia on self-knowledge. Self-knowledge means first of all recognizing the part our passions play in our opinions, our biased choices and judgements. There is no progress towards truth, which alone "makes us free" (John 8. 32), unless we are able to recognize the very large part prejudice plays in our decisions.

But self-knowledge can also mean, even if here this knowledge is more subtle and delicate, knowing the secret and unconscious motives of our actions. How many "vocations", for example, are only the "projections" of an aggressive and avenging super-ego, itself the result of excessive parental authority. I dare say God can use even that though it must be put to the test as much as possible, and the one in question must see himself clearly or at least more clearly. It is one thing to have or not to have a vocation; it is another to be so mentally twisted that one fears marriage, not because of a vocation to celibacy but simply because of an unconscious fear arising from a vengeful and powerful super-ego. Even if he cannot rise above these, it is not out of place for each one, while taking care not to push the interpretation too far in a matter which only God sees clearly, to know his more obvious limitations, his more obvious psychological defects and the habitual manifestations of certain anxieties which are often revealing as to their origins and motives. The remainder of such an analysis is a technical matter and belongs to specialized medicine. Such a treatment is not in place here. But since each individual is his own doctor for the ordinary actions of life, each is also called, in the same measure, to be his own psychologist. Knowledge and hygiene of the soul is no less necessary for the manifestation and full expression of liberty. We are no longer under the law but under the grace of the Holy Spirit. The progressive "interiorization" of these external laws, customs, social conventions, as well as the spontaneous use of our own psychic reactions, our abilities and lack of abilities, our limitations, presuppose from the start that we do not underestimate them.

Although no knowledge of laws could free us without love, the law of the Spirit which does make us free is primarily and essentially the law of love poured into our hearts by the Holy Breath which has been given us.

Jesus, in fact, has left us after having fulfilled his pasch. He is absent. But his Holy Breath has passed over us. It is in us. It lives in us as it lived in Jesus. It will raise up our mortal bodies too. It is thus that the Breath of God which hovered over the waters long ago will complete his work. In one single Breath, in one single respiration, God who is all in all, will silently proclaim in the hearts of all men the Love who is God.

SELECT BIBLIOGRAPHY

In this series:

CHENU, M. D., O.P.: *Is Theology a Science?*

LEFEBVRE, Gaspar, O.S.B.: *The Spirit of God in the Liturgy.*

PIAULT, Bernard: *What is the Trinity?*

AQUINAS, St Thomas: *Summa Contra Gentiles,* translated by Fathers of the English Dominican Province, London, Burns Oates, 1923–8; *Summa Theologica,* Volume 1, London, Burns Oates, and New York, Benziger, 1948.

ARENDZEN, J.: *The Holy Trinity,* New York, Sheed and Ward, 1937.

CONGAR, Yves, O.P.: *The Mystery of the Church,* London, Geoffrey Chapman, 1960.

GARDEIL, Ambroise, O.P.: *The Holy Spirit in Christian Life,* St Louis, Mo., Herder, 1953.

GARRIGOU-LAGRANGE, Reginald, O.P.: *The Trinity and God the Creator,* St Louis, Mo., Herder, 1952.

HENRY, A. M., O.P. (Editor): *God and His Creation,* Volume 2 in the *Theology Library,* Cork, Mercier Press, and Chicago, Fides, 1956.

KLEIN, F.: *The Doctrine of the Trinity,* New York, Kenedy, 1940.

LEBRETON, J., S.J.: *History of the Dogma of the Trinity,* New York, Benziger, 1939; *The Life and Teaching of Jesus Christ,* London, Burns Oates, and New York, Macmillan, 1958.

SCHEEBEN, Mathias J.: *Mysteries of Christianity,* St Louis, Mo., Herder, 1946.

SHEED, F. J.: *Theology and Sanity,* London and New York, Sheed and Ward, 1947.

SMITH, George D. (Editor): *The Teaching of the Catholic Church,* London, Burns Oates, and New York, Macmillan, 1948.

TANQUEREY, A.: *A Manual of Dogmatic Theology,* New York, Desclée, 1959.

VONIER, Dom Anscar: *The Spirit and the Bride* reprinted in the *Collected Works,* Volume 2, London, Burns Oates, and Westminster, Md., Newman Press, 1953.

The Twentieth Century Encyclopedia of Catholicism

The number of each volume indicates its place in the over-all series and not the order of publication.

Date Due

MY 3 '61	FEB 19 '98		
MY 22 '61	MAR 18 '98		
JE 22 '61			
AG 1 '61			
JY 17 '62			
AG 14 '62			
DEC 3 '62			
JUL 2 '63			
JUL 10 '63			
89.8T 00			
SE 6 '65			
JY 6 '66			
MAY 15 '72			
OC 18 '85			
OC 10 '86			
NO 15 '88			
MAY 1			
NOV 3 0 1990			
ℬ	PRINTED	IN U. S. A.	